THE H(UMAN) MBA

Lessons from the Classics of Literature and
Philosophy you don't learn in business schools

J. ANDRÉ DE BARROS TEIXEIRA

THE H(UMAN) MBA

Lessons from the Classics of Literature and
Philosophy you don't learn in business schools

J. ANDRÉ DE BARROS TEIXEIRA

THE H(UMAN) MBA

Lessons from the Classics of Literature and
Philosophy you don't learn in business schools

First published in Portugal in 2020 by Solidserenity Lda.

Copyright © by J. André de Barros Teixeira

Designed by Sara Portela dos Santos | ssantos.eu

August 2020
ISBN 978-989-54893-0-5

SolidSerenity Lda.
Alcabideche, Portugal
www.thehumanmba.com

To my father, GMT (1919-2020), who taught me the first lessons in the importance of thinking and reason, and the belief in human dignity and science.

To my first teacher, TG, with whom I learned how to smell and enjoy the pages of a new book.

To my first Math's teacher, JRG, for making me discover beauty in objectivity.

To my first real boss, RIFM, who showed me it was possible to be a values-based leader.

To my family, for the infinite patience and perennial encouragement.

For many years I have been confronted with the fact that my love and respect for the letters and the humanities were to be hidden from the public if I were to succeed in a business career. I have been surrounded by some incredibly "effective" managers who can, without hesitation, identify, describe and create material value at the expense of humans and humanity. The more I progressed in my professional life, with all its ups and downs, successes and failures, the more I came to realise that without the refuge of the classics, I would have committed an intellectual hara-kiri. With the help of the amazing lessons found in the great books, I was able to understand and accept that there is no contradiction in being principled and effective at the same time. Above all, they taught me to **never sacrifice principles and always preserve humanistic values**. Other leaders and managers I had the pleasure to interact with were a living example of it. The selection that follows is a simple yet representative sample of a collection of classics that is infinitely larger. It is nothing but a call to thinking, in a world so full of action. It will hopefully elicit in the spirits of the student or the accomplished business leader, the interest in great reading and deeper thoughts. The suggested metaphors and analogies are just teasers. As you build your own book of purpose, bringing humanism to your managerial or leadership styles, **you will find your own connections and the ones that will enrich your holistic experience**. This book would not have been possible without the incredible contribution of many of my co-workers, teachers, inspiring coaches, facilitators, etc. It would be unfair to mention a few names, but they know who they are, and they also know how grateful I am to them for being passengers on the same journey with me. This book has also been made possible by the multiple-way translations and language advice from Isa Mara Lando and Mauro Lando.

J. André de Barros Teixeira followed a very rich career in six continents as an executive, vice-president, president and general manager in multinationals, such as Coca-Cola, Campbell's, Interbrew, and Goodman Fielder, as an expert consultant for Globalpraxis, and in government scientific research with CSIRO, in areas ranging from R&D and innovation to operations, business, and technology commercialization. André is now an entrepreneur, a partner in two European start-ups, an expert in the Science/Marketing interface, a consultant and keynote speaker in the areas of innovation, multiculturalism in business, global development, motivation, storytelling, ideation, the future of foods, humanistic values in management, international education, etc. He is a mentor of CEOs and executives, a member of different boards, and an executive professor in business schools in Europe and South America, including the Antwerp Management School of the University of Antwerp, in Belgium, and the University of Fortaleza, Brazil. He is a former chairman of the board of the International School of Brussels, where he is now an honorary trustee. With a background in Philosophy, Chemistry, Food Science, and Business, André is the author of "**THE H**(uman)**MBA**", a humanistic management and leadership development program based on the Classics. He created a technique for idea generation for innovation that has so far been used in more than thirty countries. He is particularly keen on the use of the humanities in technical and business education and his other interests are French and Spanish-American literatures, English theatre, jazz and classical music, the philosophy of science, Fernando Pessoa, Leonard Cohen, languages, Soviet architecture, the Chinese cultural revolution, World War II, contemporary art and all things Italian, including its cuisine, its wines, and AS Roma. Having lived in North and South America, Eastern and Western Europe, Asia, Africa and Australia, he is a multilingual, Brazil-born, UK-educated Belgian citizen, who now lives between Portugal and Belgium and has four children and two grandchildren.

❝A man who speaks 10 languages, who has lived in Europe, Asia, the Americas, and Australia, who holds graduate and postgraduate degrees in Food Science, Philosophy, Chemistry and Business, who can read in their original language Rousseau, Sartre, Spinoza, Dante, Shakespeare..., La Gazzetta dello Sport, the Financial Times, Die Welt, De Telegraaf, El País, the Folha de São Paulo, Le Figaro... ..... can only be an exceptional man, one who is genuinely interested by others. I have been a colleague and a friend of André's for 30 years. He is unique, deep, innovative, a humanist with an extraordinary sense of humor, capable of presenting a business plan in Atlanta to the Chairman of The Coca-Cola Company while giving a psychological portrait of the Russian President, to the disbelief of the audience. This great book can only be written by a person who deeply understands human chemistry, what makes people better, unique and different. In today's environment, it is a must to have someone of André's caliber putting the subject of "Human Enterprise" back in the agenda of the business school system.

PHILIPPE MARMARA
Senior Partner, SVP
Globalpraxis - Barcelona, Spain
www.globalpraxis.com

This is a most original, creative, enlightening and truly fun book about Wisdom. The author, which I am tremendously lucky and proud to name a friend for many years now, is a living example of a wise man, a walking book of wisdom. One could fill large rooms with books on MBA's; there is none like **THE H**(uman)**MBA**. The innovative angle to approach understanding and learning, by standing on the shoulders of great philosophers, thinkers, writers… is stunning. And shocking too, because of the radical lessons learnt, unfolding hardly called upon knowledge, lifebelts commonly available and deep-rooted value added to our current lives, dilemmas and professional future challenges. André wholeheartedly opens his personal rucksack loaded with experiences, observations, successes and failures from all the very many professional assignments he took up around the globe, for each of us to grab in, taste and sense, and acquire. His serial entrepreneurship ventures, management and leadership of multinational units and companies, his rich life as a scholar, son-partner-father and friend, colour each chapter of this book. It is, however, his uncurbed passion for innovation, his creative mind and soul, and how all this shape a more whole and wiser human being, that stands out in this work.

Since wisdom isn't innate but can be acquired through experience -over the years- André's new approach to contribute to the nature of our learning processes, including MBA's, offers an entirely new set of insights, sheds a different light on our traditional norms and (professional) behaviours, and acts as a stronghold for those wanting to grow more authentic and in search of humanity.

In the combination of a most refreshing journey alongside giant historic thinkers, the academic rigour carefully built by the author, the many evoked 'moments of truth' through self-reflection gently spiced with humour shows the Master behind this piece of art.

This book is without any doubt a gem of innovative thinking and writing, a tremendous driver for an 'understand and learn' appetite, and a revelation of how wonderful philosophy can be in approaching contemporary personal and business challenges.

BIE DE GRAEVE
AMS Corporate Membership Network
Antwerp Management School - University of Antwerp, Belgium

THE H(uman)**MBA** is the kind of book that is going to connect to the best of yourself and will help you find innovative, effective and amazing ways to impact your life and the lives of others. Through a profound philosophical knowledge ranging from science to art, this book helps you understand the values of a meaningful leadership and prepares you to make courageous and authentic decisions. It rescues lessons from the past, teaches you through experience and serves as a guiding light to a brighter future. **THE H**(uman)**MBA** reflects André's way of dealing with his career and personal life: tradition, innovation and positive impact balanced in the brilliant mind of a generous and great human being.

LILIA MAIA DE MORAIS SALES
Professor, Researcher and Vice-President for Graduate Programs
University of Fortaleza, Brazil

INDEX

PREFACE

I met J. André de Barros Teixeira in 2015 at a conference where he presented some of his experiences leading business or driving innovation programs in large corporations around the world, from Europe to America to Australia. His insights were shaped by a wealth of experiences as executive, entrepreneur, innovator and academic with the most outstanding ability to extrapolate deep truths from the complexity of the world we live in.

Since then, André has been the most generous individual - with his time and in sharing his thoughts. The time spent in his home office or talking over fantastic meal or coffee, talking about innovation, management and life is something that I treasure dearly. He has given lectures to my students, he contributed to my book, but most of all he has helped me grow as a scholar and as person, showing me how to step away from the little things that are demanding what seems urgent attention in our lives, and trying to identify what drives human behaviors and the big picture.

There is lots to love about this book that really makes you step back and reflect. And there are three aspects of the book that I find incredibly powerful.

First, history does repeat itself. Situations that are new to you are not new to the world. They have been dealt with in some shape by others at different points in times. Some aspects of human behaviour may change. Think about how we have changed as a result of having a smartphone, a computer in our hand. They also make you realise that there are some frameworks and principles that hardly change, and once you grasp them deeply they will guide your understanding of the world, the way you relate to others and the impact you can have at a much deeper level.

From personal growth to managing dilemmas, coping with failure, the power of experience, there is no single building blocks in the book that you cannot relate to, be inspired by and be guided by.

In "Learning from the lives of others", André reminds us that "regardless of how unique we think we are, there are always examples out there of lives that resemble our own." As a young manager today, you might have the chance to work for several different companies during the length of your career. And in each of them, you might not have seen enough previous situations to know how to deal with uncertainties, adversities and opportunities. As a seasoned executive, you might have worked only in two or three other companies. That is a fairly limited sample for learning from an academic perspective. When you add to that sample the experiences of many other and how they have dealt with situations, then you have your own group of mentors, or as I would call it, your own Advisory Board to consult in times of need. And in that Board, I always include a Stoic person, able to stick to a humanistic vision while facing difficulties, fully committed to live in the present, committed to the future but not slave to the past.

Second, André's deep reflection and ability to extrapolate and communicate insights that I experienced in my conversations with him have been truly transported in the book. It's not unusual that authors write books for themselves, to make sense of things. I feel André has written this book for YOU, for each of us. Each chapter is intentionally short. You are in charge to make connections between topics you need to use daily in our business life and your personal life as well.

Learning happens when you do interpret the information yourself, and in this case the books, when you tease out connections and your curiosity makes you look for these authors and books quoted. This approach is very much humanistic and quite different from what you would do in a typical business course, it encourages deep reflections and action, looking at the past while making commitment to yourself about the future. This is one of the most powerful approaches to really empower yourself to be a better human being, a better manager.

As André says in "Seeking meaning", "we must drop the net, reflect about the essence, the cause and the consequences of what surrounds us and seek their meaning." And this book achieves just that. With carefully selected words, blocks and flow, you are guided through a search for meanings for your professional and personal life.

Third, we are obsessed with how new technologies are going to change the world, make our lives better, or take jobs away. We are excited by every new product launch. We often forget that first of all technology is a human matter, it is about the new meanings that it brings to our life and our business.

In the last chapter, André invites you to write your own book of purpose, built on those humanistic values that become anchors to help with the definition and elaboration of that very purpose in life, and not only purpose in your careers. Leaders today must be humane, oriented by values of tolerance, diversity, and sustainability. Leaders today must be an improvement to the leaders from the past. They have much technology, productivity hack, knowledge than previous generation, but they also have more distractions. And those leaders who combine fundamental principles, deep reflection and a humanistic approach are very much likely to be in demand and have a competitive advantage in a world where everyone else is busy with "a faster processor."

THE H(uman)MBA is the kind of book that you are going to read most probably in one go, almost holding your breath to the end. You can't wait to see all the clusters, the building blocks and which books have been selected. Then, if you are like me, you'll print out the graphs and place them well visible in your office, so you can glimpse at them when you need guidance. And then you will go back, read the book again and do the reflections activities. And then you'll go back over and over again, in times in which big decisions await your wisdom, in times in which you might need and want to step back from the decisions and think about the bigger consequences, how they pan out over time.

The more you read and study and the more disciplines you get close to, from business to philosophy to literature and science, you'll appreciate there is a limited set of principles that drive discovery, decision making and execution. These principles, that André has beautifully extrapolated for you, will be in your toolkit in navigating and helping to create our new world, tools as important as the business frameworks or productivity software you use every day.

Massimo Garbuio, PhD
Associate Professor, The University of Sydney Business School
Sydney, May 25, 2020

INTRODUCTION

? How can you as a manager or leader be successful, results-oriented, focused on the bottom line, deliver on shareholders' expectations etc., etc. and, at the same time, keep your sanity, your life in balance, continuing to grow, being sensitive to other people's aspirations and positioning yourself in the world at large in a way that the social impact of your presence goes beyond just the immediacy of business results?

? How can you be "great" without necessarily being misunderstood or hated or both?

? How can you remain human when all the demands tend to be so inhuman?

? How can you go "from good to great" and still be good at the end?

The lessons from the Classics are there not only to be pragmatically applied but, above all, to be savored. As we approach the period when the baby boomers begin to consider retirement and the millennials are confronted with having to re-tool themselves to compete against artificial intelligence and robots, it is highly appropriate to examine the giants whose shoulders many have used to see further and to think better.

Many of the topics in **THE H(uman)MBA** program (HMBA), are not taught at business schools. However, some of them are highly pertinent to the drama and, sometimes, comedy lived by managers worldwide on a daily basis.

After a long career in business in large multinationals the world over, it downed on me that many of the situations I was confronted with on a daily basis could easily be classified under a few broad headings taught at school. However, situations such as the need to show resilience, the ability to identify obsessions of all kinds, the management of dilemmas, etc., were never taught in a business school context.

In clustering those topics under such broad headings, it was possible to tackle them better. To find texts that would encapsulate the need to understand them provided a soothing intellectual pleasure.

Every topic has a reference to a book. Every topic has excerpts from those books and a guideline for discussion in a group or individual reflection. Fifteen minutes per topic and the ensuing reflections will be of enormous value to fundamentally put everything in perspective. Every topic has its own questions. They are questions we can ask ourselves in order to reflect about the importance of learning for understanding as a critical step in the path towards success.

Such an exercise may not get you promoted, but it will certainly open your eyes to different angles of humanistic thought. It may not make you a better manager, but the reading of the recommended books will certainly make you a better person. If that does not land you a better job, it will surely help you have a better life. People with a life well lived will be better managers after all. While success does not necessarily bring about happiness, happiness is success.

3 "CLUSTERS"

36 TOPICS YOU DON'T LEARN AT SCHOOL

39 BOOKS TO HELP YOU INTERNALIZE THE CONCEPTS WHILE ENJOYING GREAT READING

1 BOOK ONLY YOU CAN WRITE.

The eight-hour programme of guided debate to deliver the full **HMBA** is available online or via a live workshop with the author.

Knowing who you are, understanding how you manage and the impact your management choices and style have on others are all essential **clusters** for developing a holistic approach to success and happiness.

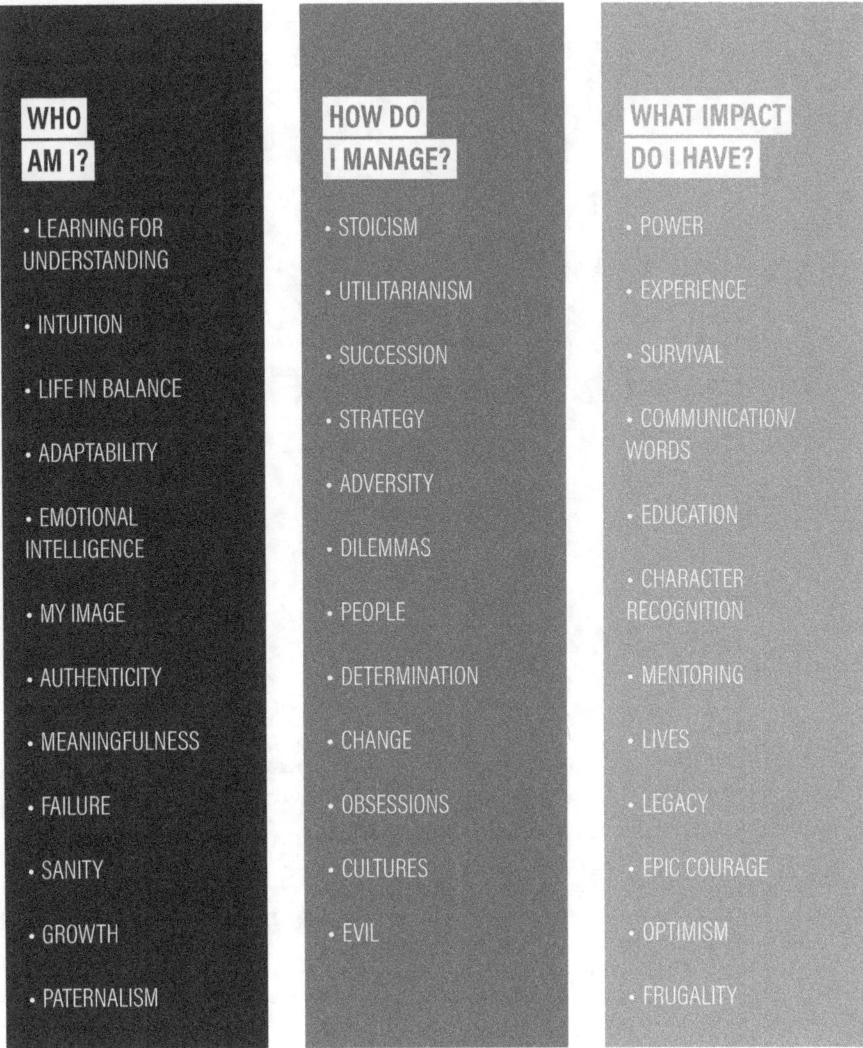

Each one of these **three clusters** has a **dozen building blocks** that form the basis of an integrative and holistic understanding of self and how others and society are impacted by our own approaches and decisions.

THE SELF PILLAR

WHO AM I?

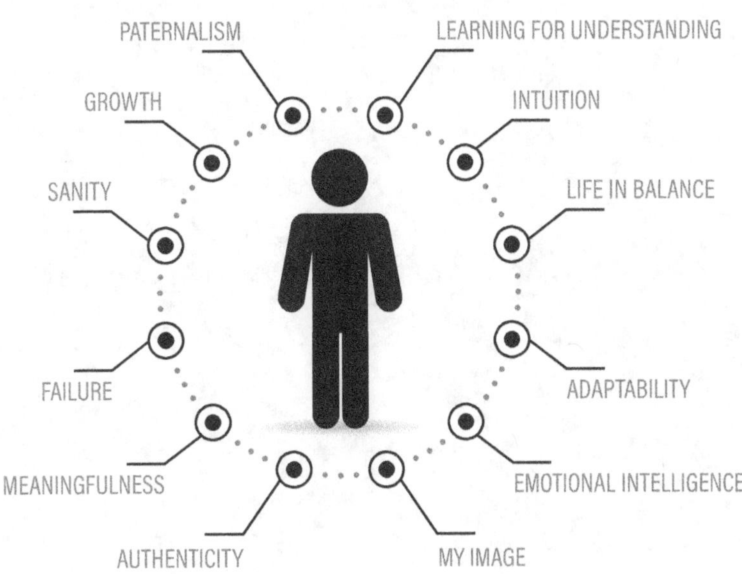

The twelve building blocks corresponding to the self pillar are:

- LEARNING FOR UNDERSTANDING
- INTUITION
- LIFE IN BALANCE
- ADAPTABILITY
- EMOTIONAL INTELLIGENCE
- MY IMAGE
- AUTHENTICITY
- MEANINGFULNESS
- FAILURE
- SANITY
- GROWTH
- PATERNALISM

THE "MANAGE" PILLAR

HOW DO I MANAGE?

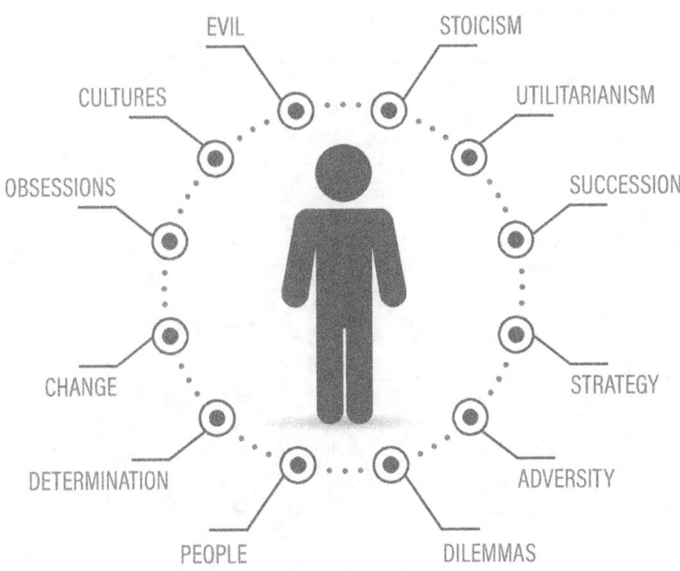

How you manage can be classified and perceived under the following dimensions, the twelve building blocks of this category:

- STOICISM
- UTILITARIANISM
- SUCCESSION
- STRATEGY
- ADVERSITY
- DILEMMAS

- PEOPLE
- DETERMINATION
- CHANGE
- OBSESSIONS
- CULTURES
- EVIL

THE "IMPACT" PILLAR

WHAT IMPACT DO I HAVE?

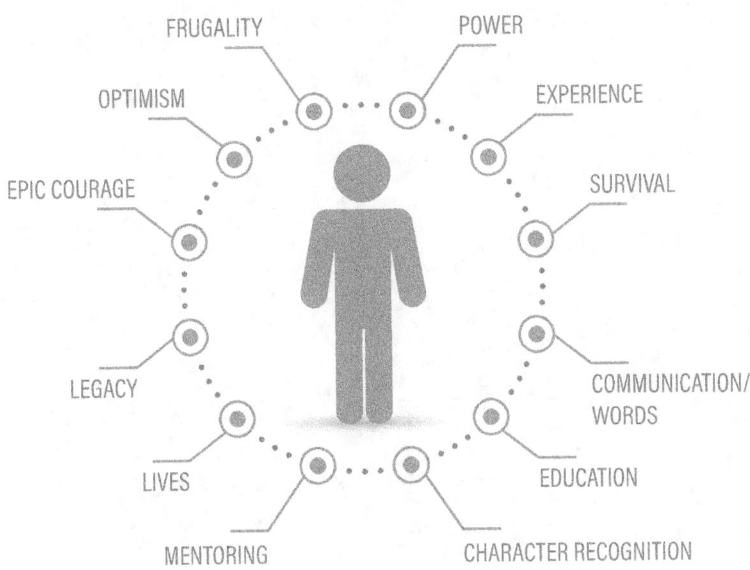

The impact you and your style of managing can have on others, the organization and society at large are captured under twelve other building blocks, as follows:

- POWER
- EXPERIENCE
- SURVIVAL
- COMMUNICATION/WORDS
- EDUCATION
- CHARACTER RECOGNITION

- MENTORING
- LIVES
- LEGACY
- EPIC COURAGE
- OPTIMISM
- FRUGALITY

Everyone aspires to be capable to **learn and understand**, using **intuition, adaptability** and **emotional intelligence** to lead a **life in balance**. While being **authentic** and **meaningful** in all we do, we seek to project exactly that **image** while striving to overcome **failures** with no **paternalism** and continue to **grow** without losing our **sanity**.

Every manager would like to show stoicism in the face of adversity, keeping a utilitarian focus on the task at hand while sticking to strategy that enables change, anticipates and manages crises with determination, empowers people and is culture proof. Every good manager will identify evil, so the practice of good can be applied to all people, regardless of the dilemmas and obsessions faced. An excellent manager will also learn early in the career to plan a healthy succession.

All this power, all this experience ought not to be used simply for survival. Education, mentoring and communication are major impacts a management style will have in an organization. The lives of people, and the recognition of their characters are going to be impacted and a style centered on an almost epic courage, coupled with a dose of rational optimism can provide a legacy of frugality of material needs and a wealth of moral and ethics.

To the thirty-six topics, three more have been added to provide the backdrop to many of the choices that need to be made. Simplicity, leadership in the spirit of law and integrity, and enough flexibility to prevent destructive pride from prevailing over reason are three more elements of reflection.

All the topics above, the building blocks of **THE H**(uman)**MBA**, can hardly be taught in business schools. The depth of reflection needed to tackle all the challenges is seldom achieved by buying "How to…" books at the airport and never opening them again after the flight lands.

Yet, we experience daily in our life as managers or leaders the enormous challenge of being the guiding light and the strategist, the general and the inspiration, the fact-based scientist and the visionary poet.

The future can be very hazy when the present is so contradictory. While juggling is a desirable skill for leaders, it is normally performed at the circus. However, in business, in public service and organizations at large, juggling should not be performed for entertainment.

Learning from experience, enlightening the mind and soul, and applying what is learned to what needs to be done are the fog light that serve as our compass and ruler.

Therefore, when the future is not so clear, that is when we need to climb onto the shoulders of giants to see it.

36 TOPICS

3 BACKDROPS
FOR REFLECTION

40 BOOKS

36 + 3 = 40?

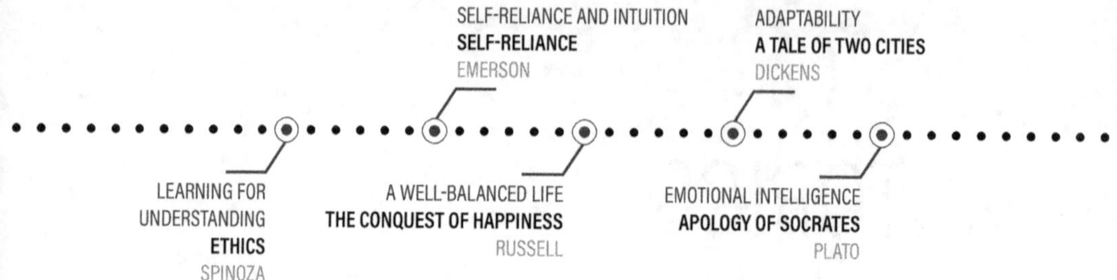

SELF-RELIANCE AND INTUITION
SELF-RELIANCE
EMERSON
ADAPTABILITY
A TALE OF TWO CITIES
DICKENS
LEARNING FOR UNDERSTANDING
ETHICS
SPINOZA
A WELL-BALANCED LIFE
THE CONQUEST OF HAPPINESS
RUSSELL
EMOTIONAL INTELLIGENCE
APOLOGY OF SOCRATES
PLATO

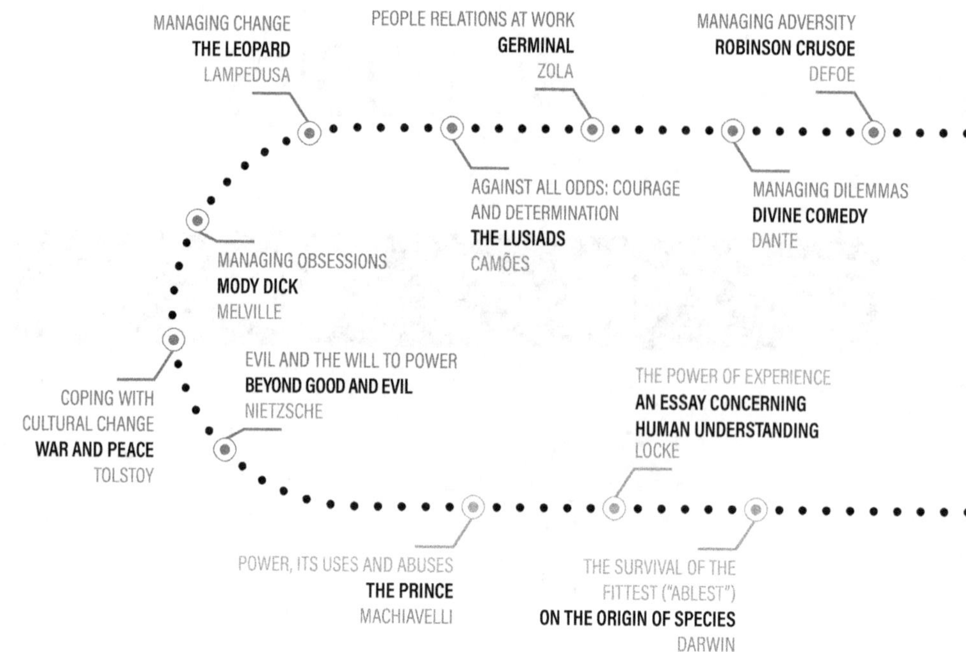

MANAGING CHANGE
THE LEOPARD
LAMPEDUSA
PEOPLE RELATIONS AT WORK
GERMINAL
ZOLA
MANAGING ADVERSITY
ROBINSON CRUSOE
DEFOE
AGAINST ALL ODDS: COURAGE AND DETERMINATION
THE LUSIADS
CAMÕES
MANAGING DILEMMAS
DIVINE COMEDY
DANTE
MANAGING OBSESSIONS
MODY DICK
MELVILLE
EVIL AND THE WILL TO POWER
BEYOND GOOD AND EVIL
NIETZSCHE
THE POWER OF EXPERIENCE
AN ESSAY CONCERNING HUMAN UNDERSTANDING
LOCKE
COPING WITH CULTURAL CHANGE
WAR AND PEACE
TOLSTOY
POWER, ITS USES AND ABUSES
THE PRINCE
MACHIAVELLI
THE SURVIVAL OF THE FITTEST ("ABLEST")
ON THE ORIGIN OF SPECIES
DARWIN

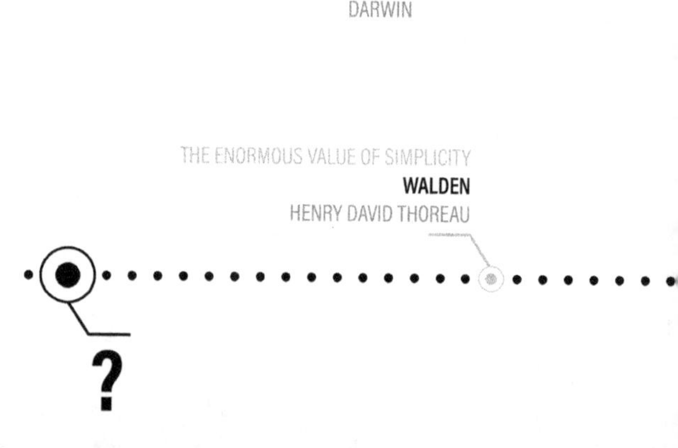

THE ENORMOUS VALUE OF SIMPLICITY
WALDEN
HENRY DAVID THOREAU
?

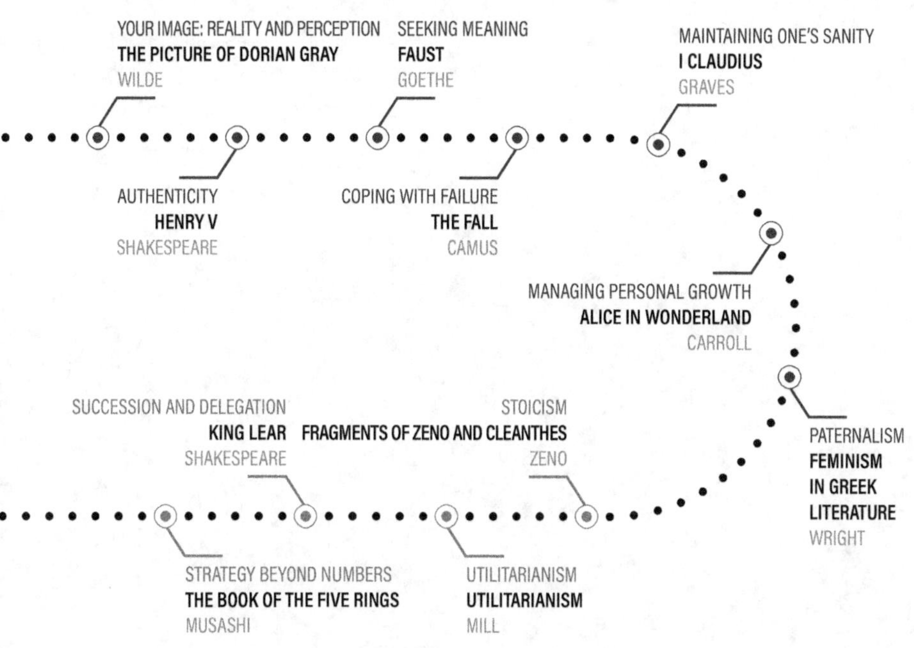

YOUR IMAGE: REALITY AND PERCEPTION
THE PICTURE OF DORIAN GRAY
WILDE

SEEKING MEANING
FAUST
GOETHE

MAINTAINING ONE'S SANITY
I CLAUDIUS
GRAVES

AUTHENTICITY
HENRY V
SHAKESPEARE

COPING WITH FAILURE
THE FALL
CAMUS

MANAGING PERSONAL GROWTH
ALICE IN WONDERLAND
CARROLL

SUCCESSION AND DELEGATION
KING LEAR
SHAKESPEARE

STOICISM
FRAGMENTS OF ZENO AND CLEANTHES
ZENO

PATERNALISM
FEMINISM
IN GREEK
LITERATURE
WRIGHT

STRATEGY BEYOND NUMBERS
THE BOOK OF THE FIVE RINGS
MUSASHI

UTILITARIANISM
UTILITARIANISM
MILL

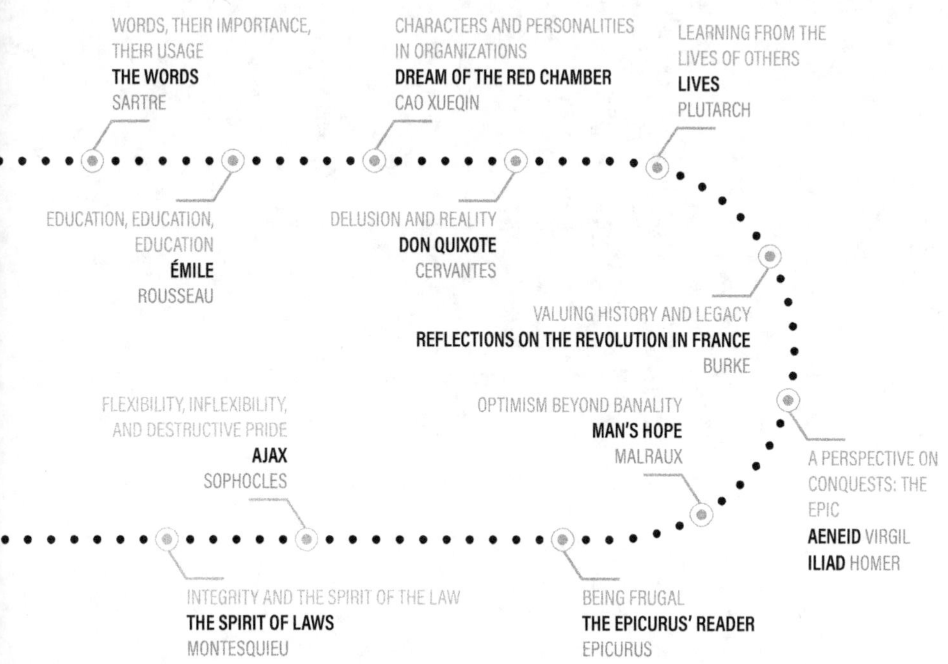

WORDS, THEIR IMPORTANCE,
THEIR USAGE
THE WORDS
SARTRE

CHARACTERS AND PERSONALITIES
IN ORGANIZATIONS
DREAM OF THE RED CHAMBER
CAO XUEQIN

LEARNING FROM THE
LIVES OF OTHERS
LIVES
PLUTARCH

EDUCATION, EDUCATION,
EDUCATION
ÉMILE
ROUSSEAU

DELUSION AND REALITY
DON QUIXOTE
CERVANTES

VALUING HISTORY AND LEGACY
REFLECTIONS ON THE REVOLUTION IN FRANCE
BURKE

FLEXIBILITY, INFLEXIBILITY,
AND DESTRUCTIVE PRIDE
AJAX
SOPHOCLES

OPTIMISM BEYOND BANALITY
MAN'S HOPE
MALRAUX

A PERSPECTIVE ON
CONQUESTS: THE
EPIC
AENEID VIRGIL
ILIAD HOMER

INTEGRITY AND THE SPIRIT OF THE LAW
THE SPIRIT OF LAWS
MONTESQUIEU

BEING FRUGAL
THE EPICURUS' READER
EPICURUS

$36 + 3 = 40$?

One of the most important books
you can read is the one
only YOU can write:

YOUR OWN BOOK ABOUT
YOUR PURPOSE IN LIFE

LEARNING FOR UNDERSTANDING

We all know that we have to learn constantly, every day. But it's not just a matter of learning – we have to really understand or, as my teachers used to say, to apprehend.

Nowadays, however, we face a permanent challenge in relation to learning. Whereas in the past there was a simple dichotomy – facts vs. fantasy – today we are witnessing the emergence of so-called "alternative facts".

Alternative facts, probably caused by the phenomenon of overlapping knowledge with information, flourish on the interface between facts and fantasy. Let's remember that knowledge is a body of collective wisdoms, organized in a relatively disciplined way and delivered to a target audience through a channel called "information".

When this channel is mistaken for knowledge – that's when alternative facts begin to prevail.

There has never been such a great need to really grasp the meaning, to actually understand what we learn, so that we can differentiate knowledge from information.

Now I would ask you to think about a situation where facts and fantasy were completely mixed up and what impact this confusion exerted on the

> *There has never been such a great need to really grasp the meaning, to actually understand what we learn, so that we can differentiate knowledge from information.*

specific circumstances in your life and your work or business at that time.

Is believing in something without factual evidence as important as reaching a conclusion based on facts and data?

One of the classic works that tells us a lot about the importance of learning in order to know and understand is Spinoza's ***Ethics***.

Published posthumously in 1677, ***Ethics*** was the masterpiece of Benedito Spinoza aka Baruch Spinoza, a Dutch philosopher of Sephardic Portuguese origin. ***Ethics*** was a fundamental rupture with medieval philosophy and established the author as one of the great exponents of rationalism in 17th century philosophy. ***Ethics*** defines the moral compass and creates the necessary conditions for true leadership, insofar as it focuses on the critical nature of understanding as the ground for good decisions. Learning to understand helps separate facts from fantasy.

 **EXCERPT FROM *ETHICS*, BY SPINOZA**

The highest activity a human being can attain is learning for understanding, because to understand is to be free.

GUIDELINES FOR DISCUSSION AND REFLECTION:

- Establish the connections between learning, understanding and freedom. How do these connections impact us.

- Facts and fantasy: Consider situations when facts and fantasy mixed up, leading to poor decisions.

- Beliefs and facts: Are both important?

NOTES, REFLECTIONS, MY THOUGHTS:

SELF-RELIANCE AND INTUITION

One of the key challenges faced by any leader, manager or director of any sort is the need to take a decision based on one's intuition when the body of available evidence points, most often, in the opposite direction.

Where can we draw the line between intuition and rational conclusions derived from undeniable data?

To be original, authentic, to avoid the temptation of just surviving in mediocrity – all of this implies a good deal of intuition, way beyond the mere ability to interpret facts and figures.

What is the point of insisting on being creative, on honoring the free spirit of intelligence if we don't use our intuition in order to become truly self-sufficient in our conclusions?

Self-Reliance, published in 1841, is an essay written by American transcendentalist philosopher and essayist Ralph Waldo Emerson. It contains the most comprehensive statement of one of Emerson's recurrent themes, the need for each individual to follow their own instincts and ideas, avoiding false consistency and conformity. In a world of big data, of fact-based decision-making algorithms, it is always refreshing to sprinkle a pinch of intuition and self-reliance.

> *What is the point of insisting on being creative, on honoring the free spirit of intelligence if we don't use our intuition in order to become truly self-sufficient in our conclusions?*

 **EXCERPTS FROM *SELF-RELIANCE/INTUITION*:**

Do not follow where the path may lead. Go instead where there is no path and leave a trail.

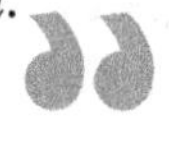

What you do speaks so loud that I cannot hear what you say.

To be yourself in a world that is constantly trying to make you something else is the greatest accomplishment.

Don't be pushed by your problems. Be led by your dreams.

 **GUIDELINES FOR DISCUSSION:**

- The tyranny of data and the reliance on intuition: Where to draw the line? How to find the balance between them?

- Being original versus accepting mediocrity.

- Reflect and discuss about situations where being original implied not accepting mediocrity.

- Doing and saying, a balancing act for leaders.

NOTES, REFLECTIONS, MY THOUGHTS:

A WELL-BALANCED LIFE

A well-balanced lifestyle has become a common concept when considering one's professional life and life in general. Anyone with a modicum of common sense would like to have a balance between their material and spiritual pleasures, between personal satisfaction and professional fulfillment, between success and happiness.

The real question is how to achieve this balance, this Zen state, this harmony with everything around us while at the same time being effective, efficient, productive, and many other characteristics that can be measured quantitatively, without losing sight of what is called quality of life.

It is even more difficult to acknowledge what others around us call a well-balanced life. This is especially true if we are in a position of leadership, eager to prioritize the collective interests and those of the organization and its more immediate results, while that desired well-balanced life is at odds, or so we think, with the best course to reach those goals.

How to reconcile something as critical as the need for results based on undisputable figures with the longing for a fuller life, brimming with inner and spiritual experiences, based on beliefs and feelings?

It is well known today that a well-balanced life

how to achieve this balance, this Zen state, this harmony with everything around us while at the same time being effective, efficient, productive makes one a better person, it prepares us better even for the more arid aspects of life, those we could call the quantitative ones. However, it was not always like this.

The transition from feudalism to capitalism was often painful, with too much emphasis placed on numbers, machines and the productivity measures that were so necessary for mankind's advancement.

The Conquest of Happiness, by Bertrand Russell, published in 1930, is one of the first comprehensive works to address the modern concept of life in balance, focusing on many aspects of the dissociation between material accumulation and the conquest of happiness. Whereas some aspects of the book are objectionable in today's more diverse and integrated societies, it is still an important call to all of those in the "rat race", to reflect and think about what constitutes real happiness.

 **EXCERPTS FROM *THE CONQUEST OF HAPPINESS:***

To be out of harmony with one's surrounding is of course a misfortune to be avoided at all costs. Where the environment is stupid or prejudiced or cruel, it is a sign of merit to be out of harmony with it.

One of the symptoms of approaching nervous breakdown is the belief that one's work is terribly important, and that to take a holiday would bring all kinds of disaster.

Worry is a form of fear, and all forms of fear produce fatigue.

 ## GUIDELINES FOR DISCUSSION:

- Everyone agrees life in balance is a good thing. Making it happen is the challenge.

- How can I be effective, efficient and high performing while striving to have a balanced life and finding inner peace?

- Do I accept life in balance in my co-workers, as much as I desire it for myself?

NOTES, REFLECTIONS, MY THOUGHTS:

ADAPTABILITY

The ability to adapt to situations, be they extreme or not, is one of the striking features of people who are successful in their careers. We have learned from Darwin that he who survives is not the strongest or the smartest, but rather the fittest, the one who adapts best.

To adapt is, essentially, being able to find solutions – often, solutions that are out of our usual toolbox.

Adapting does not necessarily mean accepting everything that occurs as if it were something natural, and always reacting differently to every situation.

Acknowledging that there may be different perspectives and finding the best way to face and solve the coming challenges, paradoxes and contradictions – that is the basis of adaptability.

A Tale of Two Cities, by Charles Dickens: Published in 1859, seventy years after the French Revolution, the novel is set in London and Paris and depicts the dramas of lives being torn between personal feelings and achievements and the broader political scene, including the reign of Terror.

who survives is not the strongest or the smartest, but rather the fittest, the one who adapts best.

 ## EXTRACT FROM *A TALE OF TWO CITIES*:

The best extract can only be the opening of the novel, so true of the time, so present to this day:

> *It was the best of times, it was the worst of times, it was the age of wisdom, it was the age of foolishness, it was the epoch of belief, it was the epoch of incredulity, it was the season of Light, it was the season of Darkness, it was the spring of hope, it was the winter of despair, we had everything before us, we had nothing before us, we were all going direct to Heaven, we were all going direct the other way-in short, the period was so far like the present period, that some of its noisiest authorities insisted on its being received, for good or for evil, in the superlative degree of comparison only.*

 ## GUIDELINES FOR DISCUSSION:

- Does everything have a flip side? Why is the business world so often immune to individual feelings?

- Can you think of situations when things looked pretty bright and pretty bleak at the same time? How do we adapt to them?

- How do the best leaders adapt to situations of significant change?

NOTES, REFLECTIONS, MY THOUGHTS:

EMOTIONAL INTELLIGENCE

The importance of emotional intelligence for one's professional success and for a more coherent and meaningful life has been well established.

Our ability to accept certain situations by understanding the emotions that make them up or condition them is increasingly essential to the success of any endeavor.

The power of ideas must always be preserved and encouraged. Not everything is pragmatic. There are very few situations where emotions do not come into play. More often than not they condition the development and consequences of projects, tasks and initiatives of all kinds.

How should we champion new ideas without necessarily eliminating the old ones? How can we prevent "post-modern" from becoming simply "pre-obsolete"? We need emotional intelligence above all else to give us the ability to anticipate the different nuances of every situation.

Plato's **Apology of Socrates**, included in the **"Judgement of Socrates"**, a translation that also contains **Crito** and the closing scene of **Phaedo**, is a good guide to multiple paths forward.

> *How should we champion new ideas without necessarily eliminating the old ones?*

Apology of Socrates, by Plato, published in the decade after the trial of Socrates 399 BCE is a reproduction of the dialogues of the judgement of Socrates and his subsequent condemnation to death. Plato, as one of his most prominent disciples wrote the account of what ensued as a form of apology.

 EXCERPTS FROM *APOLOGY OF SOCRATES*:

It is the mark of an educated mind to be able to entertain a thought without accepting it.

Strong minds discuss ideas, average minds discuss events, weak minds discuss people.

The secret of change is to focus all of your energy, not on fighting the old, but on building the new.

 *Wonder is the beginning of wisdom.*

 **GUIDELINES FOR DISCUSSION:**

- The issue of principles. How principled should organizations be?

- The power of ideas. How can we focus on them rather than just on their application?

- How can we make sure that even if the new supersedes the old, the latter is not necessarily destroyed or erased?

NOTES, REFLECTIONS, MY THOUGHTS:

YOUR IMAGE: REALITY AND PERCEPTION

Who am I? What do others think of me? What image do I project? What image of me is perceived by others? The study of reality and perception forms the basis of many studies in different fields of philosophy and psychology.

Also, in the world of business and organizational structures – admittedly, intellectually less sophisticated – the issue of perception of who we are or who we would like to be is a recurring theme in dramas and even tragedies that take place daily in the corporate environment.

The top hierarchical positions, which so many people aspire to, almost always bring along an enormous dose of image worship. To distinguish reality from perception and to make perception something as close as possible to reality are features of a sound mind in an intelligent manager.

Reading **The Picture of Dorian Gray** makes us think about the dimensions of reality and its perception.

The Picture of Dorian Gray, by Oscar Wilde, was published in book format in 1891. Dorian Gray is the subject of a full-length portrait by an artist who is enchanted by Dorian's beauty; he believes that Dorian's beauty is largely the reason responsible for his new style as a painter.

> *the issue of perception of who we are or who we would like to be is a recurring theme in dramas and even tragedies*

Introduced by the painter, Dorian meets an aristocrat, and he becomes fascinated by his hedonistic view of the world, one where beauty and sensuality are the only worthy things in life. Then understanding that his beauty will dwindle, Dorian wants to sell his soul, to make sure that the picture, rather than he, will age and fade. The wish is granted, and Dorian proceeds to lead a libertine life of varied and amoral experiences, while staying fresh, young and beautiful; all the while his portrait ages and records every sin.

EXCERPTS FROM *THE PICTURE OF DORIAN GRAY*:

Be yourself. Everyone else is already taken.

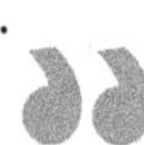

Experience is the name everyone gives to their mistakes.

Nowadays people know the price of everything and the value of nothing.

 **GUIDELINES FOR REFLECTION OR DISCUSSION:**

As brief guidelines for reflection or discussion, I suggest the following themes:

- Is perception always reality?

- How can we focus on reality and be fact based, without losing sensitivity to all things beautiful in our daily lives?

- When does the cult of the image affect the focus on reality?

NOTES, REFLECTIONS, MY THOUGHTS:

AUTHENTICITY

There are no words to describe the depth of appreciation of the human condition provided by the works of the great English bard.

Leadership in its authentic form is the light that guides us all to a peaceful and safe harbor. Authentic leadership provides daily examples of keeping that light on at all times.

Henry V, a play by William Shakespeare, believed to have been written in 1599, is an account of events around the battle of Agincourt (1415) during the Hundred Years' War, when the English, led by a young king, defeated the French against all odds. The remarkable scene is the night before the battle, when Henry V, disguised as a common soldier, visits the English camp to show solidarity to his soldiers and to gauge their motivation. The speech of the night of St. Crispin, before the battle itself, is a call to arms of gigantic proportions and a hallmark of authentic leadership. A leader who never lost sight of his human and fragile condition, Henry V is the quintessential case of leading by example.

Authentic leadership provides daily examples of keeping that light on at all times

 ## EXTRACTS FROM *HENRY V*:

*We few
We happy few
We band of brothers
for he today
That sheds his blood
with me
Shall be my brother.*

*Uneasy lies the head that
wears a crown.*

*Every subject's duty is the King's; but
every subject's soul is his own.*

 ## GUIDELINES FOR DISCUSSION:

- How does an authentic leader distinguish him (her) self from other types of leaders?

- Is leading by example enough?

NOTES, REFLECTIONS, MY THOUGHTS:

SEEKING MEANING

If we could ever combine a clarity of purpose in our lives with the finding of meaning in everything we do, it would be possible to say that we were living life to its fullest, and virtue would be holding hands with us.

Seeking meaning ought to be a constant driving force. When finding it, then it becomes imperative to find the meaning behind finding meaning and so on.

In our daily grind, with thousands of soundbites, hours of staring at screens, hundreds of emails, distractions of all kinds, with information jumping up and down in front of our eyes, preventing us from seeing knowledge, being meaningless is quite easy.

How can we make sure we have not become slaves to the permanent catwalk of information in front of us? Like Chaplin with his spanner in "Modern Times", trying to keep pace with the speed of the production line, we hold on to our smartphones as if they were butterfly nets, trapping every single useless piece of anecdotal evidence we can find.

We must drop the net, reflect about the essence, the cause and the consequence of what surrounds us and seek their meaning

We must drop the net, reflect about the essence, the cause and the consequence of what surrounds us and seek their meaning. We may never find it in its entirety, but the process will give us a perspective that will bring us closer to virtue.

Faust, by Goethe, first appeared in print format in 1790. It is a two-part tragic play and one of the most significant works of German literature and a world classic. Faust is an aristocrat who sells his soul to the devil in exchange for having all his wishes granted while he is on Earth. The pursuit of knowledge and the counterpoint of mysticism and magic form the essential backdrop to what is a major philosophical play. The meaning of knowledge, the purpose of life and aspects of virtue, love and the dichotomy of good and evil are all part of the very rich tissue of the book's construct.

 EXTRACTS FROM *FAUST*:

> *By nature, we have no defect that could not become a strength, no strength that could not become a defect.* 

> *Many people take no care of their money till they nearly come to the end of it, and others do just the same with their time.*

> *A man sees in the world what he carries in his heart.* 

> *What we don't know is really what we need and what we know is of no use for us whatever...* 

 GUIDELINES FOR DISCUSSION:

- What does it really mean to "sell one's soul to the devil"?

- Do all ends justify all means?

- How can one be meaningful and yet deliver results and perform, and be effective? Is there a contradiction?

NOTES, REFLECTIONS, MY THOUGHTS:

COPING WITH FAILURE

We are hardly prepared to deal with one of the most frequent events in our lives as leaders or managers: failure.

We fail almost as frequently as we succeed, yet we are bombarded daily with the notion that failure is an indictment on our ability, our intelligence or our integrity.

I have failed many times in my career. Many plans never materialized. Many aspirations were never fulfilled. Many dreams never saw the light of the day. Notwithstanding all that, without the failures I experienced I would never be the person I became; I would never learn some of the best lessons of my life.

Failure taught me to be humble, to accept that most of the blame in negative situations ought to be put on my own shoulders and to move quickly towards a re-invention of myself, so that I could experience other types of success. Without failures, I would have never lived certain new types of success.

The notion of winning or losing, so frequent in sports analogies as applied to business situations, is an oversimplification of the broad dimension of failure, its acceptance and the transformation that must ensue.

without the failures I experienced I would never be the person I became; I would never learn some of the best lessons of my life.

It is not just about losing or winning, as many negotiation skills classes in the business school like to teach us. It is a much wider dimension of moving away from the frivolity of our own ego and accepting, absorbing and incorporating the amazing lessons learned when we fall.

The Fall, by Albert Camus, is a philosophical novel published in 1956, with confessional monologues to a stranger by the main character, a judge who, after years of a very successful life and career, fell from grace. Various themes, such as truth, the meaning of life, innocence and crisis permeate throughout the book and are a constant reminder of the cycles of life.

 EXTRACTS FROM *THE FALL*:

I have to admit it humbly, mon cher compatriote, I was always bursting with vanity. I, I, I is the refrain of my whole life, which could be heard in everything I said. I could never talk without boasting, especially if I did so with that shattering discretion that was my specialty. It is quite true that I always lived free and powerful. I simply felt released in the regard to all the for the excellent reason that I recognized no equals. I always considered myself more intelligent than everyone else, as I've told you, but also more sensitive and more skilful, a crack shot, an incomparable driver, a better lover. Even in the fields in which it was easy for me to verify my inferiority – like tennis, for instance, in which I was but a passable partner – it was hard for me not to think that, with a little time and practice, I would surpass the best players. I admitted only superiorities in me and this explained my good will and serenity. When I was concerned with others, I was so out of pure condescension, in utter freedom, and all the credit went to me: the love I felt for myself would go up a degree.

GUIDELINES FOR DISCUSSION:

- Do we fail when our career fails?

- Think of examples of people who failed in their careers and went on to reinvent themselves.

- What is the best approach to manage failure in a project or initiative?

NOTES, REFLECTIONS, MY THOUGHTS:

MAINTAINING ONE'S SANITY

"Am I crazy or what?"

How many times have we heard or mumbled to ourselves that phrase? The easy answer is that indeed, everyone else around may be getting crazy and we are the only ones with any degree of sanity.

It is so incredibly easy to transfer the label of insanity to the organization at large, even sometimes using generic descriptions, such as, "Human Resources are a joke", "Marketing wants the impossible", "Those R&D nerds are just delaying it", so on and so forth.

How do you survive when you think that insanity surrounds you? The streetwise guy would say that you have to lie low, carry no money and run fast.

For many folks, the definition of survival is simply the maintenance of a job or a position. There is more to it though. To be able to continue to grow, to be meaningful and to enjoy life amidst all the difficulties is a key skill that needs to be studied and developed.

I Claudius, by Robert Graves, published in 1934, was written in autobiographical format and together with ***Claudius, the God***, is a historical novel about the life and reign of Claudius, the Roman emperor. The grandson of Augustus, he

How do you survive when you think that insanity surrounds you?

survived many of the troubled periods and tribulations of Rome, due to the fact that he was considered a fool. He stammered, had a limp and a few other nervous tics and ended up becoming emperor after most of his family entourage had been murdered. An intellectual, a historian, a close friend of Herod, King of the Jews, Claudius' life was an example of survival against all odds, with a love of the letters and history amongst those who were mainly playing political games.

EXCERPTS FROM *I CLAUDIUS*:

There are two different ways of writing history: one is to persuade men to virtue and the other is to compel men to truth.

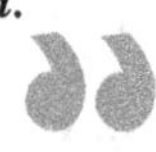

I am supposed to be an utter fool and the more I read the more of a fool they think me.

I, Tiberius Claudius Drusus Nero Germanicus This-that-and-the-other (for I shall not trouble you yet with all my titles) who was once, and not so long ago either, known to my friends and relatives and associates as "Claudius the Idiot", or "That Claudius", or "Claudius the Stammerer", or "Clau-Clau-Claudius" or at best as "Poor Uncle Claudius", am now about to write this strange history of my life; starting from my earliest childhood and continuing year by year until I reach the fateful point of change where, some eight years ago, at the age of fifty-one, I suddenly found myself caught in what I may call the "golden predicament" from which I have never since become disentangled.

GUIDELINES FOR DISCUSSION:

• When almost every event around you become somehow illogical and nonsensical, what shall you do to maintain your sanity and continue to be productive and effective? Share or reflect about examples of what can be done and how.

NOTES, REFLECTIONS, MY THOUGHTS:

MANAGING PERSONAL GROWTH

There is a time in our lives when we cease to be children and teenagers and embark on adulthood. Then, our growth as individuals and our career development become, at least theoretically, strictly our own responsibility. It is very common though, to see many grown-ups, even professionals waiting for someone or some organization to provide them with all the elements of personal development, as if they were pre-teens waiting for their parents to lead the way.

When these elements are not forthcoming, then the blaming game is triggered, and we begin to develop the false impression that we are no longer responsible for our own failures.

Which way to go? When to do what we think we need to do? What is the most effective way to move forward? Sometimes the answers are not so obvious. Procrastination becomes the norm and waiting for a redemption turns into a way of life.

The answers to all those questions are all within reach and most of them depend exclusively on ourselves and our ability to listen to other people's advice and orientation.

Managing time, understanding the "space" you occupy, realizing the relativity of your own dimensions and those of your job or business, all of that can be learned and practiced.

then the blaming game is triggered, and we begin to develop the false impression that we are no longer responsible for our own failures

Alice in Wonderland, by Lewis Carroll, published in 1865, written as a children's book, has become a major example of nonsense literature. Alice's passage from childhood to adolescence poses a number of challenges from both strategic and tactical viewpoints, not unlike what is experienced by individuals as they develop their skills and competences within an organization. The series of metaphors, colorful characters, wisdoms, situational analyses and unexpected twists and turns can be an amazing parallel to the need we all have to manage our personal growth.

 **EXCERPTS FROM *ALICE IN WONDERLAND*:**

If you don't know where you are going any road can take you there.

"My dear, here we must run as fast as we can, just to stay in place. And if you wish to go anywhere you must run twice as fast as that."

"I don't think…" then you shouldn't talk, said the Hatter.

"Begin at the beginning", the King said, very gravely, "and go on till you come to the end: then stop."

GUIDELINES FOR DISCUSSION:

• Read each of the above quotes carefully and think about situations in your career development when they could have been useful. Share examples of when they were not followed and the unexpected consequences.

NOTES, REFLECTIONS, MY THOUGHTS:

PATERNALISM

If there is one aspect of a business career I will always envy in the current generations, as opposed to what I experienced in the 80s through the next forty years is the fact that diversity in all its forms has become the norm and not the exception.

When I look back at the beginnings of my own journey through many countries, offices and job positions, I cringe to remember the role played by paternalism in shaping work relations and in breeding injustice.

By paternalism I mean all forms of it, more specifically male paternalism as a vector of discrimination against women.

For someone who was 16 in 1968 while Paris was in flames with the students' protests, 18 in 1970 when Woodstock shaped music festivals forever, it was easy to expect that in 1978 while entering the workforce I would experience the evolution of habits and the role of women in society.

Far from it! In spite of all the changes, the stereotypes and archetypes of the curvy secretary with a V-cut blouse, a writing block in her hand walking away from the boss' office were very much in vogue.

the stereotypes and archetypes of the curvy secretary with a V-cut blouse, a writing block in her hand walking away from the boss' office were very much in vogue

We had come a long way from the 50s and 60s, but old habits die hard.

In the early 80s my managers were mostly born in the 20s or the 30s. They grew up in societies where the woman who worked outside of the household was still the exception. They tended, therefore, to duplicate that pattern in the workplace.

We have come a long way but, this is a battle that will never be completely won. It is highly critical that we continue to create, enable and elaborate on mechanisms of integration that ensures diversity at all levels.

The role of women, for example, has changed significantly but, it is never enough to emphasize the importance of aiming at full equality. Offices, factories, organizations are much better places today than they were only a few decades ago. Much of that improvement can only be attributed to the critical contribution of women.

In order to understand why it has taken human beings, men in particular, so long to accept the need to change, we can go back to classical times when women were perceived quite differently from their optics today.

Feminism in Greek Literature – from Homer to Aristotle, by F.A. Wright, published in 1923, is a scholarly account of the role of women in ancient societies, through the interpretation of the writings of classical Greek writers, poets and philosophers. From the understanding of mythology to the depiction of women as inferior creatures, it is possible to identify some of the most recurrent practices of male paternalism in the business world. It is even possible to extrapolate the reflections about paternalism in the strict sense of the word, as a leadership style in which a male leader utilizes the power conferred upon himself to dominate, protect, punish, and reward in exchange for tacit acquiescence from his subordinates or followers, to models of paternalism that affect political systems, state sponsored giving and other forms of false security. As Margaret Thatcher said, "More than they wanted freedom, the Athenians wanted security. Yet they lost everything – security, comfort and freedom. This was because they wanted not to give to society, but for society to give to them. The freedom they were seeking was freedom from responsibility. It is no wonder, then, that they ceased to be free. In the modern world, we should recall the Athenians' dire fate whenever we confront demands for increased state paternalism". However, paternalism in its basic form, expressed in discrimination against and exclusion of women from certain levels in organizations continues to be a widespread phenomenon in societies misguided by religious fundamentalism, as well as the more developed and enlightened corners of the world.

In order to understand why it has taken human beings, men in particular, so long to accept the need to change

EXCERPTS FROM *FEMINISM IN GREEK LITERATURE – FROM HOMER TO ARISTOTLE*:

To revenge the gift of fire to men, Zeus resolves to make a woman. 'I will give them an evil thing', he says; 'every man in his heart will rejoice therein and hug his own misfortune'. Accordingly, Hephaestus mixes the paste and fashions the doll. Athena gives her skill in weaving, Aphrodite 'sheds charm about her head and baleful desire and passion that eats away the strength of men.' Finally, Hermes gives her 'a dog's shameless mind and thieving ways.' Then the doll is dressed with kirtle and girdle, chains of gold are hung about her body, spring flowers put upon her head, and she is sent down to earth. 'A sheer and hopeless delusion, to be the bane of men who work for their bread.

In Aristotle's time, for reasons which this brief survey of Greek literature has, perhaps, made plain, the facts of women's nature were certainly not sufficiently comprehended. Euripides and Plato are almost the only authors who show any true appreciation of a woman's real qualities, and to Euripides and Plato, Aristotle, by the whole trend of his prejudices, was opposed. His mistake was that he failed to realise the moral aspects of feminism. A nation that degrades its women will inevitably suffer degradation itself. Aristotle lent the weight of his name to a profound error and helped to perpetuate the malady which had already been the chief cause of the destruction of Greece.

GUIDELINES FOR DISCUSSION:

• Reflect on the archetypes of male paternalism that have plagued business and organisations for centuries. Think of examples of what can be done today to empower women and to proactively define a more equitable system.

• How to identify, diagnose and combat male paternalism at work?

• "Feminist" men. Do they make better leaders? Why?

NOTES, REFLECTIONS, MY THOUGHTS:

STOICISM

Among the main features I found in people who impressed me for their courage and determination, those who were able to stick to their humanistic vision when facing difficulties of all kinds, stoicism always struck me as the key factor, the one that really made a difference.

In one's professional career, as in life in general, being stoic means resisting everything that is negative and making the positive side prevail.

One of the healthiest effects of the presence of stoic people in an organization is the fact that they usually lead by example.

They adequately distinguish between three types of situations: those when one needs to accept something; those when being challenged is part of the process; and those when rejection is the only acceptable response.

Individual reasoning and collective thinking are not always connected, and it is almost always up to the stoics to find these connections.

Stoics think positively and, despite being committed to the future, they live wholly in the present and are not slaves to the past.

The rational side prevails in their attitudes, their behavior and their philosophy of life.

What would have made you resist the temptation to abandon an idea, a project, an initiative?

Think about how stoicism could have helped you in some situations where you felt it was inevitable to give up. What prevented you from being a stoic? What did you lack? What would have made you resist the temptation to abandon an idea, a project, an initiative?

Now think about conquering yourself, your fears, your anguish, your anxieties as the basis for conquering of the world.

Stoic philosophy has influenced a large number of people throughout the centuries, who had the privilege to learn from the teachings of their masters. Stoicism is the driving force for a resilient approach, for willpower and for the earnest desire to live in harmony with the universe. Many of the world's great leaders and thinkers credit Stoicism for a sense of comfort and balance, both in their personal and professional lives. Unfortunately, only a few Stoic writings have survived until our days. Some of Stoicism's greatest thinkers were emperor Marcus Aurelius, Seneca, Epitetus, Cicero, and Zeno of Citium

 **EXCERPTS FROM ZENO, *FRAGMENTS OF ZENO AND CLEANTHES* AND OTHER STOICS:**

Man conquers the world by conquering himself.
(Zeno of Citium)

If one does not know to which port one is sailing, no wind is favourable.
Seneca

It is not what happens to you, but how you react to it that matters.
Epictetus

I will now follow Reason, wherever she shall lead me.
(Cicero)

Never let the future disturb you. You will meet it, if you have to, with the same weapons of reason which today arm you against the present.
(Marcus Aurelius)

When you arise in the morning, think of what a precious privilege it is to be alive – to breathe, to think, to enjoy, to love.
(Marcus Aurelius)

GUIDELINES FOR DISCUSSION:

• Find the link between individual reasoning and collective reasoning. How can they be different? What to do when your own reasoning does not align with the collective reasoning in the context of a company or organization.

• Think about instances when there was a need for acceptance of your ideas and when some of these ideas were challenged or rejected. What can we learn from Stoic philosophers to maintain our convictions?

• Stoics lead by example. Mention some situations in which you set the example and others followed you.

NOTES, REFLECTIONS, MY THOUGHTS:

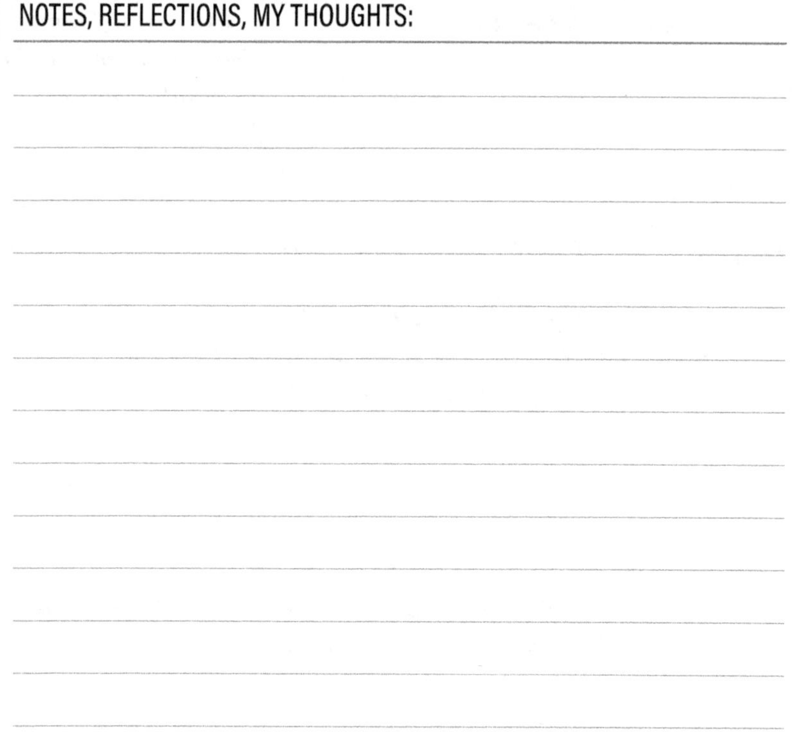

UTILITARIANISM

One of the most widespread ideas in organizations and in business at large is the notion of the collective good, and the fact that people expect the collective good to always prevail.

One of the most interesting dilemmas found in the business world is: How can one be original and, at the same time, pragmatic?

What are the limits of utilitarianism? To what extent do we have to make the collective good prevail? Do we always need to keep our feet firmly on the ground, even when our eyes are on the stars?

Identifying passions and beliefs in an organization is an effective way of defining and managing the collective good, without the risk of alienating the best individual ideas, those that can lead to something truly original.

As defined by the **Merriam Webster** dictionary, Utilitarianism is a doctrine where the useful is the good and the determining consideration of right conduct should be the usefulness of its consequences; ***specifically***: a theory that the aim of action should be the largest possible balance of pleasure over pain or the greatest happiness of the greatest number of individuals.

The **Cambridge** dictionary defines it as the

How can one be original and, at the same time, pragmatic?

system of thought that states that the best action or decision in a particular situation is the one that brings most advantages to the most people.

The classical work on **Utilitarianism** is the book of the same name by John Stuart Mill, published in 1863. In spite of the fact that it was the subject of many critical attacks throughout the centuries, Utilitarianism played a significant role in making utilitarian ethics popular and has become a very influential articulation of liberal humanistic morality from a philosophical viewpoint.

EXCERPTS FROM J. S. MILL'S *UTILITARIANISM*:

One person with a belief is equal to ninety-nine who have only interests.

The fatal tendency of mankind to leave off thinking about a thing when it is no longer doubtful is the cause of half their errors.

He who knows only his own side of the case knows little of that.

Originality is the one thing which unoriginal minds cannot feel the use of.

GUIDELINES FOR DISCUSSION:

• The idea of the prevailing collective good. How can we preserve individual happiness if the collective good deviates from the individual opinion itself?

• Identifying beliefs and passions in the organization.

• Being original while keeping the focus on being pragmatic for results. Examples from daily life. Discuss, reflect.

NOTES, REFLECTIONS, MY THOUGHTS:

SUCCESSION AND DELEGATION

Why, we wonder, is it so difficult for us to plan for succession, especially our own succession? Would it be because we want immortality, or at least long for it, even though death is one of the few certainties we have?

Planning our own succession becomes even more complex, for it is tantamount to admitting our own mortality, our limitations and the notion that we are replaceable.

Truly great men and women, especially those in leadership roles, are typically humble people, aware that they are nothing but a link in a long chain.

Many, however, even those who leave indelible marks in history, end up falling in the trap of a false sense of immortality, a craving for being constantly told that they are irreplaceable, that there is no one else like them.

A leader who cares about his succession builds it from day one "The king is dead – long live the king!"

The sycophants, the court eunuchs, are there to feed this false sense of perennialism. They surround the leader like bees in a hive, buzzing around him, supporting everything he has to show or say. In return, their egos get the feeling of being powerful simply for being close to power.

Or, in a more banal and recent analogy, it is like a Ferrari salesman who feels like a millionaire just for rubbing shoulders with those who can afford a luxury car.

A leader who cares about his succession builds it from day one. "The king is dead – long live the king!" – they are well aware that this is the tune of organizational change.

How many powerful leaders, how many people with a false sense of power have I met along my career path who felt all-powerful, immune to the necessity to delegate both tasks and even power itself, unable to mention their own inevitable succession, even if it was imminent?

Where to find inspiration to better manage this challenge?

King Lear, by William Shakespeare, an early 17th century tragedy, depicts the descent into madness of a king who based his succession plans on flattery by his three daughters. One of the most often neglected aspects of corporate life, succession ought not to live only on the agendas of boards, but rather be part of every leader's concerns. Avoiding the temptation of flattery is one of the most difficult tasks faced by leaders in any organization. The boundary between madness and reason is very flimsy when the sweet song of flattery carries the leader away. Compassion and forgiveness are also found as a theme in King Lear and are so very central to authentic, humanistic leadership.

 EXCERPTS FROM *KING LEAR:*

Have more than you show, speak less than you know.

Nothing can come of nothing.

GUIDELINES FOR DISCUSSION:

- When should a good succession plan begin?

- Is the false sense of immortality the first sign of madness prevailing over reason?

- Are succession plans only for top leaders? If not, how to put forward one's own succession plan?

NOTES, REFLECTIONS, MY THOUGHTS:

STRATEGY BEYOND NUMBERS

Not much to say in a chapter that deals with a profound truth, seldom practiced by many managers: There is more to strategy than numbers.

Strategic thinking requires a lot more than staring for hours at a spreadsheet and seeing correlations between numbers that the normal brain cannot justify.

There is more to strategy than numbers.

The Book of Five Rings, by swordsman Miyamoto Musashi, published around 1645, is a classical Japanese book on martial arts whose text has been used by many people in the West as an analogy to strategic thinking applied to business situations.

 **EXCERPTS FROM *THE BOOK OF THE FIVE RINGS:***

Timing is important in dancing and pipe or string music, for they are in rhythm only if timing is good. Timing and rhythm are also involved in the military arts, shooting bows and guns, and riding horses. In all skills and abilities there is timing.... There is timing in the whole life of the warrior, in his thriving and declining, in his harmony and discord. Similarly, there is timing in the Way of the merchant, in the rise and fall of capital. All things entail rising and falling timing. You must be able to discern this.

In strategy there are various timing considerations. From the outset you must know the applicable timing and the inapplicable timing, and from among the large and small things and the fast and slow timings find the relevant timing, first seeing the distance timing and the background timing. This is the main thing in strategy. It is especially important to know the background timing, otherwise your strategy will become uncertain.

In strategy your spiritual bearing must not be any different from normal. Both in fighting and in everyday life you should be determined though calm.

GUIDELINES FOR DISCUSSION:

- How can you train your brain to be conscious of timing and its importance in strategy?

- Imagine or share with others, situations when better timing would have changed the course of events.

NOTES, REFLECTIONS, MY THOUGHTS:

MANAGING ADVERSITY

There are very few situations where one can clearly see both the best and the worst in people's character, as when they must face adversity.

Typically, we can mention anticipated adversities or, in contrast, the sort of adversity that strikes us as an immense surprise, a gigantic asteroid that falls right on our heads. Whatever the case, the way we respond to adversity is a kind of thermometer that measures our ability to find the right path, the most appropriate strategy.

Fatalism, blind belief in solutions devoid of any concrete proposals or analysis of consequences are all useless and fall into the category of hope – and as we all know only too well, **hope is not a strategy**.

Where can we find shelter to learn how to face adversity with determination, and perceive what must be done?

Robinson Crusoe, by Daniel Defoe, published in 1757, considered by many the first English novel, has been translated in as many languages as the Bible. Many themes are recurrent throughout the novel and the adversity of the situation lived by the main character only leads to those themes coming to the surface: Religion, spirituality, family, hierarchy, slavery, etc.

and as we all know only too well, hope is not a strategy.

 ## EXCERPTS FROM *ROBINSON CRUSOE*:

> *Fear of danger is ten thousand times more terrifying than danger itself.*

> *Expect nothing and you will always be surprised.*

> *It is never too late to be wise.*

 ## GUIDELINES FOR DISCUSSION:

- How to define the fine line between hope and strategy?

- Is adversity necessary in order to harden character?

- Do leaders need to be wise or just practical?

NOTES, REFLECTIONS, MY THOUGHTS:

MANAGING DILEMMAS

If there is a subject matter that I would have loved to take with me to a business school on a deserted island, it would be the management of dilemmas. The process of easy decision making can be managed by simple calculations and results indicators.

More often, however, such decisions are not so crystal clear and considerations around the various options consume an apparently endless amount of time. We are reminded here of some famous dilemmas in life, some odd situations where we have to decide between two apparently absurd options. It is the classic case of, as they say in Portuguese, "I don't know if I should marry or buy a bicycle" ...

Learning from the consequences of dilemmas that have been already solved may be one of the most important building blocks of a manager's skills development.

Where to find that book? At what airport can we find that book by that obscure author who teaches us how to be happy, how to solve dilemmas and how to make lots of money in the process? Well, this book does not exist.

So, once again, we will find solace in the classics.

It is the classic case of, as they say in Portuguese, "I don't know if I should marry or buy a bicycle"

Divine Comedy, by Dante Alighieri, was completed in 1320, one year before his death, and it is considered the most significant work of Italian literature. The vision of the afterlife, as propagated by the Catholic Church of the time, takes the narrative through Dante's journey through Hell, Purgatory and Heaven. It helped established Tuscan as the base of modern Italian language. Full of symbolism and written in the form of "canti" (chants), it has 33 canti per each period, plus an introductory "canto". Virgil, the Roman poet, is Dante's guide through Hell and Purgatory and Beatrice, his idealized woman, the guide through Heaven.

 EXCERPTS FROM *DIVINE COMEDY:*

The hottest places in hell are reserved for those who, in times of moral crisis, maintain their neutrality.

The secret of getting things done is to act.

The path to paradise begins in hell.

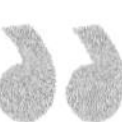

 ## GUIDELINES FOR DISCUSSION:

- Discuss two examples: One where a dilemma was easy to solve, and another when it was much harder.

- What does a leader need to do to "see" heaven when he/she is deeply grounded in hell?

- How to best learn from decisions made after confronting dilemmas?

NOTES, REFLECTIONS, MY THOUGHTS:

PEOPLE RELATIONS AT WORK

Relationships with one's work teams is one of the biggest challenges leaders and managers must face. Keeping the necessary level of realism while simultaneously finding a way to motivate people, without false promises or illusions, defines the archetype of humanism in a manager.

Germinal, by Émile Zola. First published as a book in 1885, it is one of the most outstanding works of French literature. A superb example of realism in literature, it describes a coalminers' strike in northern France in the 1860s.

Relationships with one's work teams is one of the biggest challenges

 ## EXCERPTS FROM *GERMINAL:*

Violence has never prospered, you can't remake the world in a day. Anyone who promises to change everything for you all at once is either a fool or a rogue! 

And then there are always clever people about to promise you that everything will be all right if only you put yourself out a bit... And you get carried away, you suffer so much from the things that exist that you ask for what can't ever exist. Now look at me, I was well away dreaming like a fool and seeing visions of a nice friendly life on good terms with everybody, and off I went, up into the clouds. And when you fall back into the mud it hurts a lot. No! None of it was true, none of those things we thought we could see existed at all. All that was really there was still more misery-- oh yes! as much of that as you like-- and bullets into the bargain!

GUIDELINES FOR DISCUSSION:

- Think of a project you embarked upon when the promises far exceeded the deliverables. What was the biggest lesson you learned?

- How can we maintain good relations with our teams and, at the same time, motivate them and keep reality alive as a bright flame?

NOTES, REFLECTIONS, MY THOUGHTS:

AGAINST ALL ODDS: COURAGE AND DETERMINATION

There is no humanism without a deep sense of aesthetic appreciation of facts, objects, behaviors and attitudes. Humanistic decisions tend to carry with them an element of aesthetics.

When all around us is bleak and dry, when the scenery is devoid of any calming lake or slow-moving distant clouds, it is when we need to resort to our own ability to dream, to fantasize and to imagine a better place.

That better place is invariably found in our own soul, in our own ability to create paradise with our imagination.

However, what is often forgotten is the fact that we will never arrive at that better place without courage or determination. The aesthetic appreciation will only thrive when the seeds of courage have been buried in the fertile ground of determination.

How else can we explain that a small nation in one of the outer corners of Europe goes out to conquer the world, spreading its culture, its language and its food to places as far apart as Africa, South America, Oceania and Asia?

When courage and determination are confronted with negative or low odds, that is precisely when they tend to blossom and influence all decisions.

what is often forgotten is the fact that we will never arrive at that better place without courage or determination.

What the beautiful epic poems teach us is that only a deep sense of humanity can provide the link between past, present and future in the perspective of the quest and finding of that lost paradise of our imagination.

The Lusiads, by Luís de Camões, published in 1572 is the most beautiful epic of the Iberian Peninsula, singing the glories of Vasco da Gama's voyage around Africa and the Portuguese colonisation of the Indies. It is the first epic poem which in its grandeur and its universal reach reflects the modern world. Camões' approach is not intellectual but aesthetic; his gods and goddesses come not from philosophy but from poetry. **The Lusiads** is considered by many to be the quintessential epic poem of Humanism.

 EXCERPTS FROM *THE LUSIADS:*

A soft king makes a valiant people soft.

For these vain honours,
all this gold,
Exalt no one:
Better deserve them
and not to have them
Than to have them and
not deserve them.

To be a lion among sheep, 'tis poor.

GUIDELINES FOR DISCUSSION:

- Debate courage and determination when odds are against you.

- Do all leaders need to be daring?

- Is courage the absence of fear or the mastering of it? Think of daily examples.

NOTES, REFLECTIONS, MY THOUGHTS:

MANAGING CHANGE

We all learn very early on in our lives that nothing stays the same for too long. As we grow up, we see transformation taking place every time we look at ourselves in the mirror. The more we look, the more we see the image of the image of the image and the very notion of the original object becomes blurred. We begin to fold various images onto the surface that we once thought would define ourselves to begin with.

It is not at all different in organizations and in the wide world of business. Those layers become so stuck to the preceding structures that, more often than not, they make us forget what was there in the first place.

Yet very few of us are really prepared for or welcoming towards change. It has been said that only wet babies ask for change. In fact, they cry for it.

The insecurity caused by the perspective of change is only smaller than the fear of change itself. However, change keeps coming, inexorably trickling in towards us on a daily basis or coming as a tsunami to destroy the status quo.

We can sit patiently as a Buddhist monk under the tree and wait for change; We can try to deny it and behave as if nothing is ever going to change; We can even pretend we love it and be the vector of change ourselves.

Yet very few of us are really prepared for or welcoming towards change.

However, nothing is as powerful as living change as a positive driver of our constant evolution. Whether it is an individual or an organization or enterprise, embracing change and shaping and defining it towards higher goals and solid values tend to be a recipe for a meaningful career or a meaningful life.

The Leopard, by Lampedusa, published in 1958, is the best-selling novel in Italian history and considered by many critics as the most significant and important novel in modern Italian literature. It tells the story of a 19th century Sicilian prince confronted with huge change in the social and political scenes, amidst revolution and civil war. The need for change and the struggle between decadence and eternity are central themes to the novel.

 **EXCERPTS FROM *THE LEOPARD*:**

If we want things to stay as they are,
things will have to change.

To rage and mock is gentlemanly,
to grumble and whine is not.

Love. Of course, love. Flames for a
year, ashes for thirty.

GUIDELINES FOR DISCUSSION:

- Why should we drive change when all is going well? How can we do it?

- Think of instances when you just complained and whined rather than acted to improve or change a situation. How can we prevent that from happening?

- If nothing is forever, how soon should change begin?

NOTES, REFLECTIONS, MY THOUGHTS:

MANAGING OBSESSIONS

If there is a psychological profile that defines the majority of successful executives in the world it is the one of compulsive obsession.

The problem with it is that, even when the intentions are good and the focus on results is disguised as true leadership, drive and priority on shareholders' interests, obsession shows its tentacles loaded with compulsion, selfishness, ego culture, and fundamental lack of humanity.

I have seen "good obsessives" and "bad obsessives", the latter far outnumbering the former. The most significant impact of their behaviour though, tended to be felt in their teams.

The "good obsessives" always find the time to explain the "why" things need to be the way they are. They are prepared to adapt, to change, to modulate their pressure on others according to the reality of intermediate points of observation of a project or task towards a common goal.

The bad ones are blinded by the dazzling vision of the final result that is yet to come, and behave as if all steps along the way were only a burden, obstacles to be overcome in order for the final goal to be attained and be attained on time and on budget, no matter what sacrifice is required.

> *obsession shows its tentacles loaded with compulsion, selfishness, ego culture, and fundamental lack of humanity.*

Many teams have drowned together with such bad skippers. In most cases, the skipper gets moved elsewhere, so as to continue to exercise their obsession where it is disguised as great drive.

Moby Dick, by Herman Melville, published in 1851 and narrated by a certain Ishmael, tells the story of Ahab, the obsessive captain of a whale boat, seeking revenge on Moby Dick, the white whale that on a previous whaling expedition bit off his leg just below the knee. A number of themes are pervasive through the book, but many critics agree that epistemology (the branch of Philosophy concerned with the theory of knowledge) is probably one of the most recurrent. Ahab's dogmatic rigidity contrasts with Ishmael's meditative open-mindedness and they form the basis of a remarkable assessment of obsession.

EXCERPTS FROM *MOBY DICK*:

Queequeg was a native of Kovoko, an island far away to the West and South. It is not down in any map; true places never are.

There is wisdom that is woe, but there is a woe that is madness.

It is better to fail in originality than to succeed in imitation.

GUIDELINES FOR DISCUSSION:

- What are the first signs of being obsessed with something?

- How can we avoid obsessions? How to best deal with those we consider to be obsessive personalities?

- Are humour and self-deprecating acceptable forms of countering obsessions?

NOTES, REFLECTIONS, MY THOUGHTS:

COPING WITH CULTURAL CHANGE

Change is painful. Pain is unavoidable. Suffering, however, is optional. Learning to deal with major changes, especially those of a cultural nature, as mergers and structural changes proliferate, is a matter largely neglected in the syllabuses of business schools.

War and Peace, by Leon Tolstoy, was first published in its definitive format in 1869 and is considered as one of the greatest universal novels of all time. The author though, did not consider it a novel or a chronicle. Many critics and readers see it as a rather philosophical work. It describes the significant changes in Russian society caused by the French invasion led by Napoleon, under the viewpoint of five aristocratic families of the time. Not unlike what happens in business when major mergers and acquisitions take place, "speaking the language of the enemy" becomes a risk and an opportunity at the same time.

> *Change is painful. Pain is unavoidable. Suffering, however, is optional.*

We can only know that we know nothing. And that's the highest degree of human wisdom.

Chance created the situation; genius made use of it.

At the approach of danger there are always two voices that speak with equal power in the human soul: one very reasonably tells a man to consider the nature of the danger and the means of escaping it; the other, still more reasonably, says that it is too depressing and painful to think of the danger, since it is not in man's power to foresee everything and avert the general course of events, and it is therefore better to disregard what is painful till it comes, and to think about what is pleasant. In solitude a man generally listens to the first voice, but in society to the second.

GUIDELINES FOR DISCUSSION:

- How do you anticipate, prepare for and make the most of an imminent merger, acquisition or restructuring of the business you work for?

- How do you anticipate and prepare for inevitable change in your own life?

NOTES, REFLECTIONS, MY THOUGHTS:

EVIL AND THE WILL TO POWER

No reflection about power and the limits to power can avoid the interface between the philosophy of power and the psychology associated with it. Human history abounds with examples of power being taken to the extremes and quite often being exercised ruthlessly.

Business, organizations, and families all suffer at one stage or the other in their trajectory from the huge impact of power.

When I look at most powerful people I came across in business, particularly those I had the pleasure (some) and displeasure (many) of crossing their paths, I realize how important it is to be prepared to understand the real meaning of power, in order to cope with it.

The irony of the story is that most people I saw as powerful at a particular period of time dwindled over the years to their insignificance. Others, quite simple people and at the time devoid of posts or titles are, to this day, powerful beyond measure, with their influence they had on me and others.

You do not need to have the so-called power in order to understand it. Quite the opposite, the observation of power, its psychological traits, and its philosophical inklings is a first step towards its understanding.

the observation of power, its psychological traits, and its philosophical inklings is a first step towards its understanding

However, it took a giant to define a new way to understand power and the will to power.

Beyond Good and Evil, by F. Nietzsche, published in 1886 is one of the most fundamental philosophical works of modern times, breaking away from traditional concepts that prevailed for many centuries and replacing them with novel ideas, including "***Will to Power***", as an explanation for most behaviors and attitudes. A manuscript with his unpublished notes and containing most of the concepts around "will to power" was released by his sister under that very title. The borderlines between the philosophy and psychology of power, as exercised by states, organizations and even families are covered by Nietzsche in his notes. It leads to a reflection on the limits of power, the limits to growth.

 **EXCERPTS FROM *BEYOND GOOD AND EVIL* AND *WILL TO POWER*:**

My idea is that every specific body strives to become master over all space and to extend its force (--its will to power:) and to thrust back all that resists its extension. But it continually encounters similar efforts on the part of other bodies and ends by coming to an arrangement ("union") with those of them that are sufficiently related to it: thus, they then conspire together for power. And the process goes on.

(Will to Power)

[Anything which] is a living and not a dying body... will have to be an incarnate will to power, it will strive to grow, spread, seize, become predominant - not from any morality or immorality but because it is living and because life simply is will to power... 'Exploitation'... belongs to the essence of what lives, as a basic organic function; it is a consequence of the will to power, which is after all the will to life.

(Beyond Good and Evil)

GUIDELINES FOR DISCUSSION:

- Are growth, domination, and elimination of opponents inevitable?

- Is there a limit to power? How to determine it?

- How to distinguish a life without will to power to one with it? Is there will to life without will to power?

NOTES, REFLECTIONS, MY THOUGHTS:

POWER, ITS USES AND ABUSES

If I had to choose a word to define the most aspirations, the greatest number of dramas enacted within organizations, the factor most often blamed for mistakes and their consequences, the biggest cause of alleged injustices, whether real or not, I would choose "power".

Becoming powerful, rubbing shoulders with other powerful people is, most often than not, the leitmotif in the dreams of many graduates from business schools. Power as defined by hierarchical positions, sky-high paychecks, social visibility and so on.

What a strange power is contained in the word "power". It leads us almost immediately to contradictions and dichotomies in the organizational imagination. Power is a curious thing. Those who hold it either exaggerate its real power or pretend not to have it. Those who do not have it either hate it or blindly envy those who have it.

Several treatises on Psychology, Sociology or Politics have been written on the concepts and variants of power. Few, however, synthesize the dimension and scope of the consequences of power in such an elegant way as **The Prince**, by Nicoló Machiavelli.

> *Those who do not have it either hate it or blindly envy those who have it.*

Published in 1532, **The Prince**, by Machiavelli, is an analysis of how to achieve and keep political power. By studying political leaders of the time, it is possible to understand the risks of absolute power and the tragic consequences of some measures of control and command.

 **EXCERPTS FROM** *THE PRINCE*:

The first method for estimating the intelligence of a ruler is to look at the men he has around him.

Since love and fear can hardly exist together, if we must choose between them, it is far safer to be feared than loved.

Where the willingness is great, the difficulties cannot be great.

It is not titles that honor men, but men that honor titles.

 **GUIDELINES FOR DISCUSSION:**

- What are the limits of power?

- Does the end always justify the means?

- To be loved or to be feared? A point to consider.

NOTES, REFLECTIONS, MY THOUGHTS:

THE POWER OF EXPERIENCE

Knowledge and experience: two concepts that are often mixed up in companies and organizations. Having one does not necessarily entail having the other.

However, many conflict situations occur because these two elements are mixed up, whether as perceived by others or when mentioned by those who believe or claim to have one of them, or both.

In today's business world knowledge and information are increasingly overlapping. On top of that, experience tends to be a source of patterns for action, rather than being phenomena that must be connected with knowledge itself. Knowledge and experience, therefore, need to become a two-way street, so that the needs and wishes of the organization and its individual components are largely satisfied.

Is the mind really a blank slate to be filled in by experiences?

Is the mind really a blank slate to be filled in by experiences?

How can we combine knowledge and experience without losing the strength that this combination can bring to a group?

An Essay Concerning Human Understanding, by John Locke, was published in 1689. It is one of the pioneering works on the rebuttal of the

Cartesian concept of innate ideas and a fundamental source of empiricism. The mind as a blank sheet paper, later populated by experience is one of his most critical propositions. The book covers many aspects of human knowledge, including language, philosophy, mathematics, science and intuition.

EXCERPTS FROM *AN ESSAY CONCERNING HUMAN UNDERSTANDING*:

> *The actions of men are the best interpreters of their thoughts.*

> *New opinions are always suspected, and usually opposed, without any other reason but because they are not already common.*

> *The necessity of believing without knowledge, nay often upon very slight grounds, in this fleeting state of action and blindness we are in, should make us busier and more careful to inform ourselves than constrain others.*

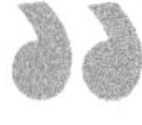

GUIDELINES FOR DISCUSSION:

- Discuss the presence and importance of knowledge and experience, and how one feeds the other in organizations at large and in the business world in particular.

NOTES, REFLECTIONS, MY THOUGHTS:

THE SURVIVAL OF THE FITTEST ("ABLEST")

Intelligence or strength are not always the determinant factors for survival. How many times have I seen in my career path highly intelligent individuals being left out in the processes of promotion, growth and recognition.

How many times have I seen the meteoric and apparently unexplainable fall of the strongest.

However, those who were the fittest those who best adapted to change, those who by chance or by fate were in the right place at the right time, those who understood how to distinguish the variations that deserved or should be retained, were always the ones who benefited most.

those who were the fittest those who best adapted to change, (...) were always the ones who benefited most

Published in 1859, **On the Origin of Species**, by Charles Darwin, is considered as the foundation of evolutionary biology. The scientific theory of natural selection was introduced in the book. Evidence from his voyage of 1830 with the ship named Beagle, plus subsequent research, scientific exchange and his own experiments were all included in the work.

 ## EXCERPTS FROM *ON THE ORIGIN OF SPECIES*:

> *It is not the strongest of the species that survive, nor the most intelligent, but the one most responsive to change.*

> *To change is difficult. Not to change is fatal.*

 ## GUIDELINES FOR REFLECTION AND DISCUSSION:

Within the world of business and organizations, we can reflect on some issues such as:

- What is the best approach to actually promoting change, rather than just accepting it?

- Blind variation and selective retention. Think about examples in your life or your organization when these phenomena occurred and their influence on the impact achieved by the selected strategies.

- Reading Charles Darwin's On the Origin of the Species broadens our horizons as we search for better solutions to our problems of adaptation to change. List a few adaptations you or your organization had to implement in order to cope with change. Compare them and identify what these adaptations had in common and on what they differed.

NOTES, REFLECTIONS, MY THOUGHTS:

WORDS, THEIR IMPORTANCE, THEIR USAGE

Words have the unique power to be, at the same time, weapons and ointment, instigators and calming element, silencing and rousing.

In the complex world of organizations, particularly those in the business space, everything communicates. If you do not communicate anything, you are communicating something.

The use of words cannot simply be manipulative, utilitarian or functional. The use of words begins with the love of words, their careful choice, their blend and their nuances and tones, very much like a palette of colors intended to paint that scenery in front of us.

Understanding our words, treating them with care and attention, celebrating the reach of their meaning and carefully lapidating them to provide whatever we want to convey in an open and honest way, is a major virtue of the humanistic leader.

The love of words begins with the love for reading. The love of books opens the curtains of our mind to a new world of meanings.

> *The use of words begins with the love of words, their careful choice, their blend and their nuances and tones, (...)*

The Words, by Jean-Paul Sartre, published in 1963 when he was 59 years old, is a masterpiece of self-analysis and the autobiography of the first ten years of his life, as he grew up among books and developed a deep relationship with them and an appreciation of the importance of language.

 **EXCERPTS FROM *THE WORDS*:**

I had found my religion: nothing seemed more important than a book. In the library, I saw a temple.

Having discovered the world through language, for a long time I took language to be the world.

GUIDELINES FOR DISCUSSION AND REFLECTION:

- Compare the importance of precision versus lengthy descriptions in business writing.

- Is there an ideal language for communicating business results? Are numbers the only language?

- How can reading impact you as a business leader?

NOTES, REFLECTIONS, MY THOUGHTS:

EDUCATION, EDUCATION, EDUCATION

No leader or manager is prepared to be a true, authentic, humanistic leader if he/she does not open his/her mind to education. Learn, learn and learn every day, from every situation, is the mantra. The transforming power of education is such that the new person, now educated in something else, needs to learn even more. Learning is a thirst that is never quenched.

Selecting the most adequate topics, courses, programs, fields of knowledge for oneself and the organizations we lead is a huge endeavor. Finding the right balance between what is needed and what brings sheer pleasure is the secret of success.

Learn, learn and learn every day, from every situation, is the mantra.

Émile or On Education, by Jean-Jacques Rousseau, published in 1762 is the essential book on the nature of education and the relationship between individuals and the collectivity they belong to. It is both a political and a philosophical work on how humans can retain their innate goodness in the face of a corrupting society. It formed the basis of a new national education system in France.

 ## EXCERPTS FROM *ÉMILE*:

> *Everything is good as it leaves the hands of the Author of things; everything degenerates in the hands of man.*

> *The ever-recurring law of necessity soon teaches a man to do what he does not like, so as to avert some other evil which he would dislike still more... this foresight, well or ill-used, is the source of all the wisdom or the wretchedness of mankind.*

 ## GUIDELINES FOR DISCUSSION AND REFLECTION:

- How can we keep on learning when we are so busy and there are so many demands? A reflection on how to draw knowledge from everything.

- What distinguishes the best development programs a business or organization can put in place? Should retention be the only concern?

NOTES, REFLECTIONS, MY THOUGHTS:

CHARACTERS AND PERSONALITIES IN ORGANIZATIONS

A radical thought is one that states that "there is no organization, there are simply characters in an organization".

Although probably not completely true, for the sake of the argument, let's imagine we were studying business organizations from the perspective of the characters present in them.

We could define their roles, their psychological profiles, their philosophy of work, the way they behave collectively versus the way their personality comes across, etc.

We would soon arrive at the conclusion that the understanding of those characters is essential for the definition of what constitutes an organization and its driving forces.

The evolution and sometimes revolution affecting families, social classes, governments, business entities or even civilizations make it for a very interesting analysis of what is important to know in order to generate a more humanistic approach to our lives as leaders and managers.

understanding of those characters is essential for the definition of what constitutes an organization and its driving forces

Dream of the Red Chamber, by Cao Xueqin, one of the great classical novels of China, was published in print in 1791 and portrays the gradual decline of a large aristocratic family in 17th century China during the Qing dynasty. The multitude of characters and the richness of detail is an inspiration towards the understanding of the human condition even within very powerful and apparently immutable structures and organizations.

 **EXCERPTS FROM *DREAM OF THE RED CHAMBER*:**

> *Truth becomes fiction when the fiction is true / real becomes unreal where the unreal is real.*

> *Although there is pleasure in the World of Red Dust, its eternity cannot be relied on. Then, these two sayings are also linked, 'there is imperfection in beauty, fortune is filled with misfortunes.' In an instant, misery can arise from the utmost happiness. People change, and so do things. At the end of the day, it is just a dream, and all circumstances will return to the void.*

GUIDELINES FOR DISCUSSION:

● Reflect for five minutes about the lives and characters of the members of an organization you belong or belonged to. How different are they? How much better would the organisation be if only we knew more about the people behind the jobs, titles and positions?

● How can we prepare for change?

● Try to remember your company, your family, or your group of friends, the way they were five years ago. Are they still the same? How have they changed? Are those organizations still the same? If not, why not? Could you imagine they would have changed the way they did in the last five years? Now, try to recognize yourself. How much have you changed?

NOTES, REFLECTIONS, MY THOUGHTS:

DELUSION AND REALITY

(MENTORING AS A TOOL)

The most common form of delusion in leaders and managers is the delusion of grandeur. When one's title on a business card or in a LinkedIn profile becomes so heavy that what it entails describes more what one does and not who one is, then it is time for a reality check.

For most artistic activities, it is quite acceptable to allow sanity and madness to touch each other from time to time. It is even possible to say that some of the most creative pieces ever produced had a touch of madness in them.

In the dry world of business though, it is estimated that sanity must prevail at all times. However, many critics have observed that madness creeps in when you least expect it.

The solitude of the leader, the fact that the leader can be surrounded by so many others, in many cases acting like eunuchs in the court of a mandarin, are all conducive to a state of madness disguised as sanity.

The best decision a leader can make, particularly if he is feeling the pressure of isolationism and his eyes are foggy with smoke screens being puffed away by so many subordinates, it is to have a mentor, a down-to-earth life mentor and not necessarily a business mentor.

The best decision a leader can make, (...) it is to have a mentor, a down-to-earth life mentor and not necessarily a business mentor.

No matter how we strive for sanity, it is also important to keep the dreams alive. What is absurd today, sometimes must be attempted in order to attain the impossible.

Don Quixote, by Miguel de Cervantes, is considered to be the most influential work in Spanish and one of the greatest works of world literature. It was published in two volumes in 1605 and 1615, respectively. The main character, Don Quixote, is a noble man who loses his sanity after reading many novels on chivalry and decides to revive it by undoing wrongs and bringing fairness and justice about. He enrolls the services of a down to earth, simple farmer, Sancho Panza, as his squire and the adventures begin. The limits between madness and reality are sometimes challenged by Quixote's delusions.

 EXCERPTS FROM *DON QUIXOTE*:

Too much sanity may be madness. And maddest of all, to see life as it is and not as it should be.

In order to attain the impossible, one must attempt the absurd.

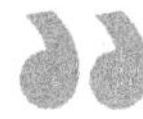

Delay always breeds danger: and to protract a great design is often to ruin it.

GUIDELINES FOR DISCUSSION:

- Discuss examples of delusion, when reality was severely affected and how it impacted final results of a project or initiative of any kind.

- Do all organizations need people with big egos? Do they all need folks with big self? Quixote and Sancho, are they complementary?

- How can we avoid procrastination in the face of a heavy agenda?

NOTES, REFLECTIONS, MY THOUGHTS:

LEARNING FROM THE LIVES OF OTHERS

Regardless of how unique we think we are, there are always examples out there of lives that resemble our own. Conversely, no matter how similar we are to people in our families, our organizations and associations, we know that we have characteristics that make us completely different from them.

There is always something to be learned from the lives of others. Nevertheless, it is not enough to simply stand by and watch other people's adventures, failures and successes. We must draw lessons and employ them in our daily lives.

it is not enough to simply stand by and watch other people's adventures, failures and successes

Lives, by Plutarch, also known as Lives of the Noble Greeks and Romans, written at the beginning of the second century AD, is a series of paired biographies of famous Greeks and Romans, so laid out to highlight common virtues and shared vices. The surviving accounts include 23 pairs, one Greek Life and one Roman Life each, as well as four single lives. The importance of understanding the lives of prominent people is highly relevant in the business world today, as many of the situations they were confronted with repeat themselves over and over again.

 ## EXCERPTS FROM *LIVES*:

Adversity is the only balance to weigh friends.

To make no mistakes is not in the power of man; but from their errors and mistakes the wise and good learn wisdom for the future.

Neither blame nor praise yourself.

It is certainly desirable to be well descended, but the glory belongs to our ancestors.

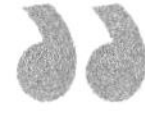

GUIDELINES FOR DISCUSSION:

- Think of someone's life from whom you learned something important. Now share with others something from your life you would like to pass on as a good example.

- Who was your best mentor? Why?

- Who would you like to mentor? Why?

NOTES, REFLECTIONS, MY THOUGHTS:

VALUING HISTORY AND LEGACY

As we propose change, as we innovate, engage in the elaboration and development of new ideas, the creative juices in our veins lead us to believe that everyone can only agree with us.

Who would dare to go against progress? Who would block our inexorable march towards a better place?

Where do we learn in the business school about the way to go when the ideology of conservatism blocks our ability to deliver the "new"?

The fact of the matter is that I have found a lot more opposition than I have met with support for ideas of innovation, to dreams of transformation.

How many business plans did I present to powerful leaders in an organization, who were simply drunk with their heavy position in the hierarchy and sitting on their imaginary thrones, that made it impossible for them to see the future?

I meet some of them now, years later, walking slowly towards their gate at an airport somewhere, and I asked them:

- Would you still oppose some of those ideas now that the very ideas have been transformed into products or services that experience so much success?

The fact of matter is that I have found a lot more opposition than I have met with support for ideas of innovation, to dreams of transformation.

The answers I normally get are quite often tantamount to an uncomfortable grumble, disguised as moaning.

Yet, the people with the new ideas, the creative minds are also to blame, for they do not know or understand the effect of history, legacy and heritage in the organization. They underestimate the power of conservatism in blocking the daring initiatives.

Reflections on the Revolution in France, by Irish statesman Edmund Burke, published in 1790, is a pamphlet that attacks the French revolution and has become a mainstay of the political philosophy of conservatism. While criticized by modern historians as flawed and in many ways inaccurate, it is respected as a classical text of political theory and critical of socialist or communist revolutions that tend to devour their own children and turn into their own opposites. When the speed of change is what it is today, it is always an intellectually healthy endeavor to learn from the past and celebrate human individuality in the face of "systems" and understand the motivations of those who resist change itself.

 **EXCERPTS FROM *REFLECTIONS ON THE REVOLUTION IN FRANCE*:**

A spirit of innovation is generally the result of a selfish temper and confined views. People will not look forward to posterity, who never look backward to their ancestors.

When men play God, presently they behave like devils.

GUIDELINES FOR DISCUSSION:

- How can we continue to propose and promote change when so many oppose it around us?

- Do we feel comfortable spending some time evaluating a bit of the past before jumping into the future? If not, why not? Is there any benefit?

NOTES, REFLECTIONS, MY THOUGHTS:

A PERSPECTIVE ON CONQUESTS: THE EPIC

There is something epic about the notion of conquest. Acquisitions and buy-outs are studied in schools under the viewpoint of strategic fit and financial sense, but deep-down they carry with them the perspective of victory that needs to be shared with the world and touted loudly as sheer greatness on the part of the conqueror.

What the classics can teach us though is that there is much more to the epic drama of the conquest. There is the human angle of it, the joy on one side, the pain inflicted on the other. It also teaches us about the sometimes ephemeral nature of the conquest itself: Today's predator becoming tomorrow's prey. Not to mention the historical revisions bringing new interpretations on the wisdom, justice or fairness of the conquest itself.

It also teaches us about the sometimes ephemeral nature of the conquest itself: Today's predator becoming tomorrow's prey.

Until not long ago, it was "perfectly acceptable" by European societies to accept and actually promote colonialism as a means of "civilizing" the world. The "Conquistadores" brought their customs, manners, clothing, so-called moral values, etc. to the "under-civilized". Nowadays some of those arguments border on the laughable.

It is critical, therefore, to learn the lessons from the great epics of ancient history, so that we can better appreciate what is happening, on a much reduced scale of course, with the business conquests of today.

The Iliad, an epic poem by Homer, probably written around 762 BCE, tells the story of the ten-year siege of the city of Troy during the Trojan War and the disputes between King Agamemnon and the warrior Achilles. ***The Aeneid***, by Virgil, written between 29 and 19 BCE, is an epic poem telling the story of Aeneas, a Trojan who became the ancestor of the Romans after travelling to what is today's Italy. Aeneas was a wandering character in The Iliad and was weaved by Virgil into a hero who is then made into the precursor of all the dynasty of emperors in Rome from the Julio-Claudian period, thus linking the latter with the gods. Both epics glorify conquest and make war noble. A parallel with the expansion of business and nations, the concept of dominance and the celebrations around them is inevitable.

EXCERPTS FROM *ILIAD* AND *AENEID*:

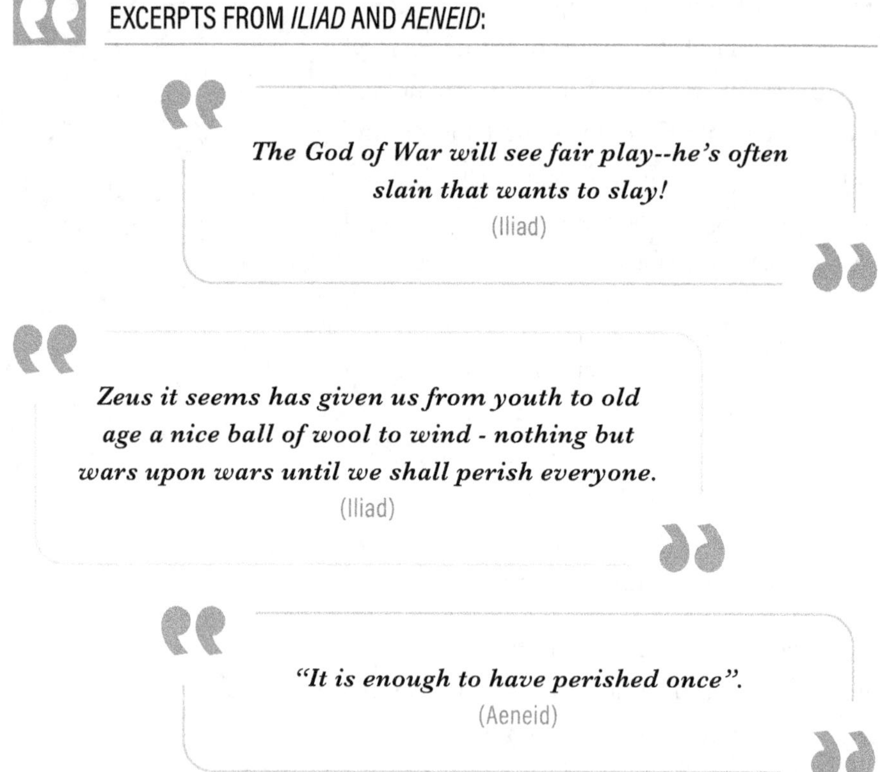

GUIDELINES FOR DISCUSSION:

- Discuss the merits of dominance, endless growth, conquests and elimination of competition in the context of finite level of resources in the world.

- Is growth the only strategy? If not, what else is there?

NOTES, REFLECTIONS, MY THOUGHTS:

OPTIMISM BEYOND BANALITY

Mindset, conviction and creed are all important elements of the development of a clear strategy. No matter how we look at it, all those points above cannot be restricted to the leader. The whole team must be imbued with that spirit.

Amazing results have been attained by teams and companies which are rather difficult to explain if we only use the tools of objectivity.

An optimist can always be found behind these successful outcomes. However, their optimism is not mundane. It normally goes through a fact-based assessment of real opportunities, a vision that goes beyond what normal eyes can see and a deep sense of the importance of mobilizing, engaging and motivating teams.

Lessons from battles won, even those that took place in wars that were ultimately lost are as powerful as are the lessons from lost battles in wars we won.

Man's Hope, by André Malraux, published in 1937 is a poignant account of the Spanish Civil War, between 1936 and the Battle of Guadalajara in 1937. The profound message of hope, based on firm convictions, against the organized forces of the state drives all characters towards rather

Lessons from battles won, even those that took place in wars that were ultimately lost are as powerful as are the lessons from lost battles in wars we won.

unlikely results in the war. Although it has been said many times that hope is not a strategy, it is always interesting to address engagement, mobilization and commitment of a group of people, when a certain dose of rational optimism prevails.

 ## EXCERPTS FROM *MAN'S HOPE*:

 *There are not fifty ways of fighting, there is only one, and that is to win.* 

 *Every situation presents at least one positive element; we must find it and work it.* 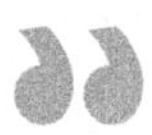

 ## GUIDELINES FOR DISCUSSION:

- When do you know you have achieved real engagement from a team?

- Is shared hope a sufficient attitude to drive engagement and motivation? If not, why not?

- How to combat fear, negative feelings and lack of action?

NOTES, REFLECTIONS, MY THOUGHTS:

BEING FRUGAL

The term epicurean has been associated with good food, good wine and the good life at large. Nothing wrong with any of those elements.

It is through intense observation though, that we notice that people who tend to be happy and leading a life of tranquillity have an interesting characteristic in common: frugality.

A certain simplicity of habits, a healthy dose of detachment from certain things material, and a focus on inner peace dominate their lives, regardless of where they stand on the hierarchical pyramid of jobs, positions or postings.

Not surprisingly, the classical Greeks already knew a lot about it…

The **Epicurus' Reader**, by Epicurus is a collection of remaining writings of Epicurus, a Greek philosopher who lived between 341 and 270 BCE. For him, philosophy had the purpose of attaining happiness and a peaceful life. This was based on aponia, the absence of pain, and ataraxia, peace and freedom from the notion of fear. A life among friends and characterized by self-reliance is a main aspect of his thinking.

It is through intense observation though, that we notice that people who tend to be happy and leading a life of tranquillity have an interesting characteristic in common: frugality.

EXCERPTS FROM *EPICURUS'* WRITINGS:

> *Death does not concern us, because as long as we exist, death is not here. And when it does come, we no longer exist.*

> *Happiness is man's greatest aim in life. Tranquillity and rationality are the cornerstones of happiness.*

> *We should look for someone to eat and drink with before looking for something to eat and drink.*

> *You don't develop courage by being happy in your relationships every day. You develop it by surviving difficult times and challenging adversity.*

GUIDELINES FOR DISCUSSION:

- How can we, in a typical business life become capable of leading a life of tranquillity and rationality? Think about some examples and share them.

NOTES, REFLECTIONS, MY THOUGHTS:

FLEXIBILITY, INFLEXIBILITY, AND DESTRUCTIVE PRIDE

Nothing can be as self-destructive as pride. Sprinkle a genius with too much pride and you will see the silhouette of mediocrity.

History is full of examples of the incredible power of pride to destroy individuals, ideas, initiatives, even states and enterprises.

Pride is to achievement what wind is to fire. Give it a little bit and the flames will burn strongly; Give it too much and it will put the fire out.

Lessons to be learned from self-destructive pride are never enough. Most cultures, many mentors, innumerable teachers tell us to be humble, to accept that we are not so powerful that we cannot learn something new. Yet, in the business world and organizations of all kinds we see the relentless procession of very proud leaders, arrogant supervisors and managers, always ready to claim credit for something they have not really done, constantly blaming those around them for anything that goes wrong.

History is full of examples of the incredible power of pride to destroy individuals, ideas, initiatives, even states and enterprises.

Very few of these flawed leaders survive long enough to tell their tales of pride. They fall gradually into oblivion, carrying with them a loaded series of lies and delusions to hide their self-destruction.

Since times immemorial many stories were told of these false heroes, whose pride destroyed their own selves.

Ajax, by Sophocles, is a Greek tragedy written on the 5th century BCE, describing the life and death of Ajax, a warrior, between the events of the Iliad and before the Trojan War. After the death of Achilles, Ajax expected to be given his armor by the two kings. Another warrior got it instead and Ajax never conformed to it, and his shame and inconformity led to suicide. Inflexibility and destructive pride were, above all, self-destructive. A great warrior was destroyed by his own pride.

 **EXCERPTS FROM *AJAX*:**

> *The long unmeasured pulse of time moves everything. There is nothing hidden that it cannot bring to light, nothing once known that may not become unknown. Nothing is impossible.*

> *Men of ill judgement oft ignore the good that lies within their hands, till they have lost it.*

> *It is a painful thing to look at your own trouble and know that you yourself and no one else has made it.*

> *If you try to cure evil with evil you will add more pain to your fate.*

 **GUIDELINES FOR DISCUSSION:**

- Build a wall. Imagine your pride on one side of it. Now imagine flexibility, acceptance and recognition of your own mistakes on the other side of it. How tall is your wall? Discuss with examples.

NOTES, REFLECTIONS, MY THOUGHTS:

- FLEXIBILITY, INFLEXIBILITY,
AND DESTRUCTIVE PRIDE

- INTEGRITY AND THE SPIRIT
OF THE LAW

- THE ENORMOUS VALUE OF
SIMPLICITY

INTEGRITY AND THE SPIRIT OF THE LAW

In many situations in business, we are confronted with legal barriers. You cannot do this because of this or because of that. Legal counsels tend to be associated with sales prevention more than with sales promotion.

Regulatory professionals are those that many mangers fear calling into a meeting because they are normally the ones throwing a bucket full of ice-cold water into the flames of some new idea or initiative.

In business teaching there is a clear need to change the focus of the legal professionals, so as to provide them with a broader and deeper role in becoming true enablers of success.

It took me a few years working in countries and regions with some of the most unstable legal systems for me to understand the amazing protection, safe harbor and business facilitation that the rule of the law provided. Before that, in systems with solid institutions, I had just taken the law for granted and never thought much about it.

You only know how good your raincoat is when it gets wet. Surrounded by the mafias in one country, living with corruption around me at all levels in others, I realized I could count on the rule of law in order to feel protected and even sheltered from the daily threats.

Legal counsels tend to be associated with sales prevention more than with sales promotion.

It is absolutely critical to reflect about integrity and the laws defining and enforcing it. It is through the law that true liberty is attained.

The Spirit of Laws, by Montesquieu, published in 1748 and prohibited by the Roman Catholic Church in 1751, is a major work on the need for political institutions to reflect the societies they represent. It is a call for a constitutional form of government with powers being duly separated and the preservation of legality and civil liberties. The concept of laws applicable to everyone is fundamental to the spirit of competition and fairness in the business world of today.

EXCERPTS FROM *THE SPIRIT OF LAWS*:

> *Liberty is the right of doing whatever the law permits.*

> *The deterioration of a government begins almost always by the decay of its principles.*

> *Democracy has, therefore, two excesses to avoid: the spirit of inequality, which leads to aristocracy or monarchy, and the spirit of extreme equality, which leads to despotic power, as the latter is achieved by conquest.*

GUIDELINES FOR DISCUSSION:

- How can we ensure that respect for the law is not just a constraint, but something that needs to be celebrated and an integral part of strategy?

- Debate a situation where integrity prevented a more immediate or more profitable result. Which lessons were drawn from it?

- "Treat everyone equally." Can this be applicable to every situation? If not, why not?

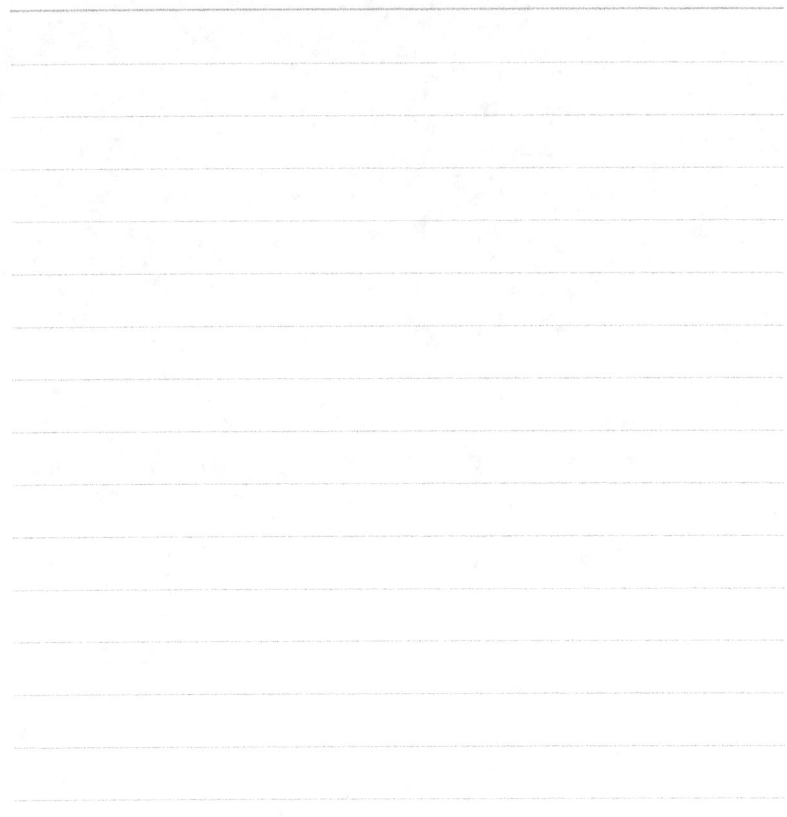

NOTES, REFLECTIONS, MY THOUGHTS:

THE ENORMOUS VALUE OF SIMPLICITY

I have often wondered what I would call this subject if it were taught in a business school: "Discomplication"? "Creating with no resources"? "Budgets with no money"?

There are many ways to look at this and they all point towards the need for simplicity in a world that is progressively becoming more complex and difficult to explain in a few sentences.

In the business world, complexity generates the need for more complexity to resolve it. Complex solutions will create some other complex problems as a by-product, and the vicious circle will only become, well,.....more complex, as it rolls down the hill.

We can obviously go on holiday, escape from it all for a while, recharge our batteries, manage our hormones through sports, go to a spiritual retreat, do some yoga or engage in meditation. They are all valid approaches to alleviate the tension of complexity and the stress of the daily grind.

However, the key word is simplicity. Finding it in every situation, both as a goal and a means is key to success.

Once again, the classics provide us with a magnificent insight on how to achieve it.

the key word is simplicity. Finding it in every situation, as both a goal and a means is key to success

Walden, by Henry David Thoreau, published in 1854, is an account of the experiment the author carried out to live in basic simplicity for two years, two months and two days, in direct contact with nature in a wooden cabin he built himself. The book is a classic in the call for simplicity and on self-reliance and helps us all to put in perspective the extreme effects of complexity in the modern world.

 **EXCERPTS FROM *WALDEN*:**

If you have built castles in the air, your work need not be lost; that is where they should be. Now put the foundations under them.

Things do not change; we change.

As if you could kill time without injuring eternity.

If one advances confidently in the direction of his dreams ... he will meet with a success unexpected in common hours.

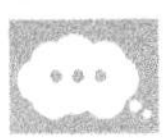

GUIDELINES FOR DISCUSSION:

- How can today's leaders, faced with so much complexity, use simplicity as an approach to solve some of the basic problems of daily business? Discuss examples of personal experiences that can be extrapolated to the organisation at large.

NOTES, REFLECTIONS, MY THOUGHTS:

A REVIEW OF THE
KEYWORDS FOR
LEADERSHIP WITH
PURPOSE

A REVIEW OF THE KEYWORDS FOR LEADERSHIP WITH PURPOSE

So, once again, let us collapse all these topics into a statement that brings them all together. All topics I wish I had learned in a business school. Luckily, they were taught to me at the much bigger, harder and fascinating school of life. All I know is that I know little, but the drive to learn is the best skill to carry.

Everyone aspires to be capable to **learn and understand**, using **intuition**, **adaptability** and **emotional intelligence** to lead a **life in balance**. While being **authentic** and **meaningful** in all we do, we seek to project exactly that **image** while striving to overcome **failures** with no **paternalism** and continue to **grow** without losing our **sanity**.

Every manager would like to show **stoicism** in the face of **adversity**, keeping a **utilitarian** focus on the task at hand while sticking to **strategy** that enables **change**, anticipates and manages crises with **determination**, empowers people and is **culture** proof. Every good manager will identify **evil**, so the practice of good can be applied to all **people**, regardless of the **dilemmas** and **obsessions** faced. An excellent manager will also learn early in the career to plan a healthy **succession**.

All this **power**, all this **experience** ought not to be used simply for **survival**. **Education**, **mentoring** and **communication** are major impacts a management style will have in an organization. The **lives** of people, and the recognition of their **characters** are going to be impacted and a style centered on an almost epic **courage**, coupled with a dose of rational **optimism** can provide a **legacy** of **frugality** of material needs and a wealth of moral and ethics.

To the thirty-six topics, three more have been added to provide the backdrop to many of the choices that need to be made. **Simplicity**, leadership in the **spirit of law and integrity**, and enough **flexibility to prevent destructive pride** from prevailing over reason are three more elements of reflection.

WRITING YOUR
OWN BOOK

No matter how much we can learn from the examples of great books, our own individual journey is guided by both knowledge and experience, not to mention instinct and intuition.

Therefore, in order to draw the specific roadmap that we will apply to our lives and careers, we must select what is relevant and meaningful to us and to couple it with what we need to learn.

Looking at the thirty-six building blocks and the three backdrops of Simplicity, the Spirit of the Law, and Flexibility, we begin by listing them:

• LEARNING FOR UNDERSTANDING	• STOICISM	• POWER
• INTUITION	• UTILITARIANISM	• EXPERIENCE
• LIFE IN BALANCE	• SUCCESSION	• SURVIVAL
• ADAPTABILITY	• STRATEGY	• COMMUNICATION/ WORDS
• EMOTIONAL INTELLIGENCE	• ADVERSITY	• EDUCATION
• MY IMAGE	• DILEMMAS	• CHARACTER RECOGNITION
• AUTHENTICITY	• PEOPLE	• MENTORING
• MEANINGFULNESS	• DETERMINATION	• LIVES
• FAILURE	• CHANGE	• LEGACY
• SANITY	• OBSESSIONS	• EPIC COURAGE
• GROWTH	• CULTURE	• OPTIMISM
• PATERNALISM	• EVIL	• FRUGALITY

• SIMPLICITY	• THE SPIRIT OF THE LAW	• FLEXIBILITY

Now, scroll all the three clusters until you find a series of three connections that appeal to you, either because you like the themes or because you feel you need to dedicate some time to learning more about them.

As you are writing something that is relevant and meaningful to you, don't worry about being logical or fitting any specific mould.

The main point is to be able to write a story that speaks to your heart and mind. Let us look at some examples.

Think of it as if you were in front of a slot machine. You make all the three columns move until they stop. The only difference is that, in this case, there is no room for random combinations. In this case, you reflected and selected what is important to you.

Let us suppose, for example, that you scrolled the three clusters and you ended up in a couple of combinations of three elements, as follows:

• LIFE IN BALANCE	• CHANGE	• FRUGALITY
• AUTHENTICITY	• DILEMMAS	• LEGACY

So, proceed to write a story of, for instance, how you can achieve a state of life in balance by changing certain habits and aspects of your daily routines while being guided by a notion of frugality not only in your personal life, but also in your organisation or business. Repeat for the other combination(s).

Go back to the books referred to for each heading. Find examples which you can apply in your task at hand. Write your own story not just by giving examples and illustrations of facts and events but, above all, by defining, describing and conceptualizing what actually is important to you as you are today and as you want to be going forward.

Explore many connections of the three clusters, always respecting the fact that they are organised under the three main headings of **SELF**, **HOW I MANAGE**, and **HOW I IMPACT**.

The following are some examples of combinations that can lead to interesting reflections as you learn from the classics to enhance your career and, ultimately, your life which is far more important than your career:

• FAILURE	• DETERMINATION	• OPTIMISM
• AUTHENTICITY	• DILEMMAS	• MENTORING
• INTUITION	• STRATEGY	• SURVIVAL
• ADAPTABILITY	• ADVERSITY	• EPIC COURAGE

A vast number of combinations can be built and, most importantly, can be changed and adapted to our own individual reality and motivations.

The selection of themes can be a function of one or more of the three typical situations:

• You wish to summarize under these overarching topics, some events in your life or career that explain how you got to where you are today and may serve as a good lesson for similar situations in the future.

• You want to capture situations, challenges or opportunities you are currently faced which require a good dose of reflection, eventually sharing with friends, family or colleagues.

• You want to anticipate scenarios in your life or career and you wish to be prepared for them, either because you need to develop certain skills or competences and/or you firmly believe some of the values captured in the topics you selected are essential for you to be happier, more effective, or whatever is your desire.

So, when you write your story connecting those three elements every time, it is an interesting proposition to repeat the exercise for each one of the selected combinations of three topics in the past, present and future.

At the same time, for each one of the time variables (past, present, future), answer the questions in the following order:

• Why? Why have I chosen this topic?

• How? How am I going to achieve it? Or how did I achieve it? Or, if in the present, how am I achieving it?

• What? What is my definition of what I want to achieve, or what I am achieving or indeed I achieved, in the future, present and past, respectively?

Some examples:

Let us suppose you selected the following:

| **Life in Balance** | Determination | Legacy |

You now revisit the material from each one of those topics and spend sufficient time reviewing your own annotations and thoughts about them.

Then you select a point in time: Past, Present or Future. If you prefer, you can choose two or all three, whatever is more relevant to you now.

For each one of the topics, answer the three questions: Why, How, and What? In that order.

Here is a real-life example for the Present:

WHY?	HOW?	WHAT?
LIFE IN BALANCE		
Life in balance is important because it gives me a sense of a broader mission in my trajectory and offers me the opportunity to live more intensely and calmly at the same time.	To achieve life in balance, I make a permanent effort to stay focused on human values, regardless of daily stress.	My time with the family is untouchable. My practice of sports and my intellectual activities are not necessarily linked to my work.
DETERMINATION		
Without determination I cannot achieve my goals of life balance.	The practice of the determination exercise requires iron discipline that I maintain under any circumstances.	Achieve goals, even when some seem impossible.
LEGACY		
If I do not leave a legacy to those who succeed me, my children or successors, life does not make sense to me.	Through a focus on the long term, I can visualize the legacy to be left, whatever the daily needs.	The transformation of the status quo. A new way to see the world. An example or "role model" to be followed.

Now, if it is relevant to you, repeat the same exercise of answering the three questions above for the Past (something you lived through that can provide you with valuable lessons) of for the Future (something you intend to do because it is important to you).

Think of it as if you are writing the script for your own movie, a roadmap, using just a ruler (to keep a sense of measure) and a compass (to orient you towards your True North).

Going back to our real-life example above, what she was asked to do was to go back to the quotes and excerpts from the classical books for each one of the topics, as well as the recommended guidelines for discussion or reflection, as shown below.

You are encouraged to read or browse through these books and, eventually, find more quotes that speak to your heart. Keeping the guidelines for reflection open, you can start drafting your own script, writing your own book of purpose.

The more personal you make your script, the more likely it will be for you to find its relevance for your purpose. Humanistic values in their vast majority are complementary and not self-excluding. So, there is no limit to the number of combinations you can create with the values that are important to you, at any stage of your career or your life.

So, back to the example where she picked Life in Balance, Determination and Legacy. It was necessary to overlay the answers to the three questions (Why? How? What?) for each one of the selected topics with the excerpts and guidelines from each one of them, as seen below:

LIFE IN BALANCE

EXCERPTS FROM *THE CONQUEST OF HAPPINESS*, BY BERTRAND RUSSELL	GUIDELINES FOR REFLECTION:
To be out of harmony with one's surrounding is of course a misfortune to be avoided at all costs. Where the environment is stupid or prejudiced or cruel, it is a sign of merit to be out of harmony with it.	Everyone agrees life in balance is a good thing. Making it happen is the challenge.
One of the symptoms of approaching nervous breakdown is the belief that one's work is terribly important, and that to take a holiday would bring all kinds of disaster.	How can I be effective, efficient and high performing while striving to have a balanced life and finding inner peace?
Worry is a form of fear, and all forms of fear produce fatigue.	Do I accept life in balance in my co-workers, as much as I desire it for myself?

DETERMINATION

EXCERPTS FROM *THE LUSIADS*, BY LUÍS DE CAMÕES	GUIDELINES FOR REFLECTION:
A soft king makes a valiant people soft.	Debate courage and determination when odds are against you.
For these vain honours, all this gold, *Exalt no one:* *Better deserve them* *and not to have them* *Than to have them and not deserve them.*	Do all leaders need to be daring?
To be a lion among sheep, 'tis poor.	Is courage the absence of fear or the mastering of it? Think of daily examples.

EXCERPTS FROM *REFLECTIONS ON THE REVOLUTION IN FRANCE*, BY EDMUND BURKE	GUIDELINES FOR REFLECTION:
A spirit of innovation is generally the result of a selfish temper and confined views. People will not look forward to posterity, who never look backward to their ancestors.	How can we continue to propose and promote change when so many oppose it around us?
When men play God, presently they behave like devils.	Do we feel comfortable spending some time evaluating a bit of the past before jumping into the future? If not, why not? Is there any benefit?

Looking at the four tables above, it is not so hard to see how one can connect the answers to the three questions to some of the inspiring elements from the great authors.

Writing up the 40th book is an exercise in patience, but also in construction, putting together all the right elements that form the basis of what will make every leader, every manager more infused with humanistic values.

We live in a world in which there is a brutal disconnect between what has been with us since prehistoric times, such as the need to survive, protect and preserve our species, and artificial intelligence, our cutting-edge technology, almost science fiction. All of this regulated and normalized by institutions created centuries ago. Living at three speeds is extremely difficult.

What will lead us to the preservation of our planet, to more just societies, to the true achievement of happiness is a high level of harmony and practice of human values, guided by leaders, business managers, professionals, intellectuals, artists or any other activities.

How many anthropologists, philosophers, social scientists do big companies hire? What is the multiplicative factor of the average salary of a brand manager in relation to the average salary of a primary school teacher? Until when will this ideology of growth at all costs?

For those in the business world, when preparing our purpose, we need an intense reflection on the fundamental importance of humanistic values, without which everything that they teach us about finance, marketing, organizational structures, strategy, etc., becomes all but meaningless. The big challenge is not simply going from "good to great", as in Jim Collins' bestseller (From Good to Great). The real challenge is to go from good to great and still remain good, human, fair, full of integrity, and so many other related values.

Going back to the classics for inspiration and guidance will make the exercise both challenging and interesting, with a healthy dose of pleasure in finding that we are all part of a long and beautiful history as inhabitants of this planet.

The transcendental aspect of the 40th book is the fact that you are its main character, its writer and publisher, editor and copywriter.

Happy writing!